Rocking the Wall
Erik Kirschbaum

Rocking the Wall

Bruce Springsteen:
The Berlin Concert
That Changed the World

Erik Kirschbaum

Rocking the Wall
Bruce Springsteen: The Berlin Concert That Changed the World
By Erik Kirschbaum

Editor: Cindy Opitz
Photos: Herbert Schulze
Copy editor: Stephen Wagley

© 2013 by Berlinica Publishing LLC
New Edition © 2014 by Berlinica Publishing LLC
255 West 43rd St., Suite 1012, New York, NY, 10036; USA
ISBN 978-1-935902-73-7
LCCN: 2013936754

Cover photo: Herbert Schulze
Cover Design: 1106 Design

Printed in the United States

All rights reserved under International and Pan-American Copyright Law. No part of this book may be used or reproduced in any manner whatsoever without written permission except in the case of brief quotations embodied in critical articles and reviews.

www.berlinica.com

For Finn, Lukas, Julie, and Steven

Thanks!

I would like to thank all those who helped turn the "crazy idea" of writing a whole book about a single rock concert into an actual published work. Thanks to Jon Landau for the insights behind the concert, and Dave Marsh for his support. Also a special thanks to Dave Graham, Daniel Remsperger, Karin Scandella, Dean Grant, Ingrid Kirschbaum, Stephen Brown, Axel Hansen, Christian Ruettger, Tom Wagner, Thomas Krumenacker, Scott Reid and Steven Kirschbaum for patiently reading earlier drafts and offering advice, a huge source of motivation.

Thanks also to Cherno Jobatey, Jochen Staadt, Peter Schwenkow, Gerald Ponesky, Yvonne Wagner, Georg Kerwinski, Conny Günther, Birgit Walter, Herbert Schulze, and Roland Claus for sharing their memories of the concert and extensive knowledge of East Germany. Thanks also to Craig Werner, Thomas Wilke, Philip Murphy, Matthias Döpfner, Miriam Dieter, and especially Danae Grant. I'd also like to express my appreciation to Olaf Zapke and Noah Barkin at Reuters for allowing me the time to finish this. A big thanks to Berlinica's indefatigable publisher, Dr. Eva Schweitzer, for her belief in this idea and for her guidance. Thanks also to Cindy Opitz for her skillful editing that helped turned a decent manuscript into a better book.

I would also like to thank the many people who contributed to the book through Kickstarter, namely Jane Driscoll, and Brian J. Bohling. And even though I don't know his name, I'm especially grateful to that long-haired Berlin taxi driver whose unbridled enthusiasm about the '88 Springsteen concert inspired me in ways he may never realize.

Erik Kirschbaum, Berlin, May 2013

Contents

Preface	9
My Trip to East Berlin	13
Introduction	19
Chapter One The Year of Upheaval	23
Chapter Two He Had a Dream	33
Chapter Three Chimes of Freedom	47
Chapter Four The Tricky Part	63
Chapter Five Journey to the Other Side	75
Chapter Six Strange Days	83
Chapter Seven Storming the Gates	91
Chapter Eight A Close Call	101
Chapter Nine Power to the People	127
Chapter Ten Tears in His Eyes	141
Postscript	151
Select Bibliography	156

The ticket stub for the 1988 Bruce Springsteen concert in East Berlin.

Preface

After a riveting Bruce Springsteen concert in Berlin in 2002, I was riding home in a taxi when the driver suddenly started chattering on about another Springsteen performance—in Communist East Berlin, back in 1988. He said that July '88 show was the most amazing thing ever, anywhere. Springsteen rocked East Berlin and rattled the whole Communist country. The concert behind the Iron Curtain happened more than fourteen years before our chance encounter on that cold October night, but the heavyset taxi driver with the thick gray beard and long scraggly hair couldn't stop raving about it.

"Yeah, I know," I said, trying to close my eyes and relax. I had just filed a Reuters news agency report on Springsteen chastising George W. Bush for bullying countries like Germany that were opposed to invading Iraq. "I've seen lots of Springsteen concerts too, and they're always amazing."

"Nein, nein, nein!" the driver replied. "No! You don't understand." That East Berlin concert was really different. There was never anything like it. More than 300,000 people watched it live, and millions more saw it on television. The whole country was shaken up. "It was the most incredible thing that ever happened in East Germany," he said, growing animated, his garlic-scented breath drifting in my direction.

For millions of baby boomers, Springsteen's music has been the soundtrack of our lives. Four decades of song lyrics are lodged in our collective memory, like "It's a death trap, it's a suicide rap, we gotta get out while we're young, cuz tramps like us, baby, we were born to run," from *Born to Run*, and "It ain't no sin to be glad you're alive," from *Badlands*. The Berlin taxi driver's uncontainable enthusiasm about that concert was contagious, and he got me wondering: Had there been something really special about that Springsteen show in Communist East Berlin?

The more I delved into it, the more I wanted to know. It was fascinating, for instance, to find out that Springsteen had the moxie to deliver a short anti-Wall speech in East Berlin. It was also incredible to read about the size and unruliness of the biggest-ever East German concert crowd—estimated to have been at least 300,000 people—and how countless thousands without tickets simply stormed the gates to get in.

And then it dawned on me—what made that particular concert so extraordinary was its date: July 19, 1988. That was less than sixteen months before the Berlin Wall fell. Could there have been a connection between the Springsteen concert, the ensuing rebellion in East Germany, and the Berlin Wall falling that no one had seen before? Might there be a direct line between Springsteen on July 19, 1988, and the Berlin Wall bursting open on November 9, 1989?

I've been wondering about these questions ever since. It seems clear to me that there must be a link between that Springsteen concert and the shifting sentiment in East Germany that led to the Berlin Wall's collapse. I got excited by the idea of trying to find out about the atmosphere and what really happened when Springsteen went behind the Iron Curtain in 1988, but there was always the daunting prospect of how I was ever going to find people who were at a concert a quarter of a century ago. That turned out to be easier than I thought because, it seems, almost everyone living in East Germany and at least in their teens in 1988 was either at the concert, knew someone who was at the concert, or heard or saw it on the radio or TV. It was almost as if time stood still on that day in East Germany—everyone seems to have a memory of it.

As good fortune would have it, Springsteen was back in Berlin in May 2012, on his "Wrecking Ball Tour," and many who attended had been at the 1988 concert as well and, like Springsteen himself on stage, were more than happy to talk about their memories. I talked to scores of eyewitnesses and a number of historians in Germany and the United States about the question of whether Springsteen's four-hour performance and fearless call to bring down the Wall might have had something to do with the revolution that began roiling in East Germany in the weeks and months that followed. Whether you believe that Springsteen's epic concert contributed to the movement that brought down the Berlin Wall depends to a certain degree on whether you believe in the power of rock 'n' roll. Among those who are convinced of those revolutionary forces is Philip Murphy, America's ambassador to Germany and an unabashed Springsteen fan. Although he wasn't in East Berlin in 1988, Murphy believes his fellow New Jerseyan did have an appreciable impact on East Germans: "I know and love Springsteen's music—and can only imagine what kind of effect the live concert must have had on East German audiences, on people living under an oppressive regime, wanting change so desperately." In the words of Jörg Beneke, who was among the hundreds of thousands who saw the concert live, Springsteen's concert was like "a nail in the coffin" for Communist East Germany, the beginning of the end.

What is beyond doubt is that Springsteen's 1988 concert in East Berlin is a glorious example of the influence that rock 'n' roll can have on people who are hungry and ready for change. This is the untold story about that once-in-a-lifetime concert in East Berlin and the role Springsteen may have unwittingly played in helping fuel a rebellion that would bring down the Berlin Wall.

Erik Kirschbaum

Mike Spengler in 2014. Foto: Chris Drukker

My Trip to East Berlin

Mike Spengler, One of the E Street Band's Horn Blowers, Remembers the Concert

After the first edition of Rocking the Wall *came out, Mike Spengler, a player in the horns section in the E Street Band in 1988, sent us his observations of the famed concert in East Berlin he participated in. We are honored and grateful to be able to publish them.*

On July 18, we flew to Berlin from Munich. We had been told that at the last minute it was decided that the band and crew would stay in East Berlin at a hotel described as "the showcase hotel for Eastern Bloc tourists." The hotel was quite the towering structure, and my room was on an upper floor over 25 stories up.... There was a color TV that received only two snowy channels.

The next morning I went down for breakfast. I met two of our crew guys on their way out. 'Don't order eggs, there aren't any," I was told, "No fresh fruit, either." I ordered a *croque monsieur* (grilled cheese and ham) that cost the equivalent of two dollars. Our road manager handled a "currency exchange." He explained that East Germany had declared a "one-for-one" rate of exchange between East and West German marks, but the real rate was more like eight East marks to one West mark. He managed to find someone who gave him four East to one West.

After eating, I decided to walk around a little. Going through the lobby was like going through Grand Central Station at rush hour. Just wall-to-wall people either sitting or standing on long lines to the front desks with a constant din of conversation. Out front a Mercedes was parked in the drive with a crowd standing around staring at it.

Crossing a city square I recall as Marx-Engels-Platz, at one point a Pan Am jet flew low overhead—low and gaining altitude. And everyone just stopped and stared up at it. I went into a large department store. Went first to the electronics department. That contained three TV sets—one small black and white, one large black and white, and one color set and also a pair of "boom boxes"—one monaural and one stereo. Plus the strangest looking contraption I'd ever seen. Imagine a kind of computer screen with a stand-alone old-fashioned typewriter (with stemmed keys!) attached. "I don't know computers, but I know a dinosaur when I see one," I thought . . .

I crossed the street to a record shop. The classical music section was pretty sparse. Twentieth-century music didn't exist. Just a couple of Mozart and Beethoven LPs. A lone exception was a cassette of Camille Saint'-Saens's Organ Symphony preformed by the Berlin Symphony Orchestra (East Berlin's equivalent to the famed Berlin Philharmonic, which stayed in the West after the division of the city). I bought it and gave a listen before we left for soundcheck and the concert . . . Later, we were introduced to Gert, who was described to us as our East German liaison. Gert was accompanied by his girlfriend, who spoke no English. I ended up sitting in front of them and we chatted. Gert told me he had originally been a French and then English teacher in a school. He loved rock' n 'roll and, when Western rock artists began performing in East Germany, a promoter wanted to hire him. The authorities told Gert he "couldn't have two jobs at the same time," so he had to choose. Which he did. During the ride, I spotted a huge sculptured bust of Ernst Thaelmann. I asked Gert who he was. "He was the leader of the Communist Party who was murdered by the Nazis and is considered a heroic martyr," was Gert's reply.

I asked Gert how this concert came about. He explained that the East German authorities wanted to make available to its youth the same kinds of things available to Western youth, and that the East German Communist Youth League, the Free German Youth (FDJ), became a kind of sponsor for these concerts with the un-

My Trip to East Berlin

derstanding that the concerts had to have an "appropriate theme." For Bruce, the FDJ proposed "Oppressed Nations."

"Not specific enough," was the reply, according to Gert.

We did our soundcheck before a growing crowd—which promised to be huge. One odd thing I recall. I spotted an American flag being waved about. I was a little concerned for whoever was waving it, but something looked a little off-kilter. I don't know why, but I actually counted the number of stars. There were 48. Could someone have broken out a flag after having stashed it for over thirty years? I wondered . . .

After soundcheck, I found myself talking with an older man who apparently was an official with the East German Cultural Ministry. Almost a walking stereotype out of an old movie. Tanned trenchcoat draped over his shoulders and holding a cigarette backwards between his thumb and forefinger. I mentioned the Berlin Symphony cassette I had bought and remarked on what a good performance I found it to be. He shrugged it off. "The Dresden Staatskapelle is our finest orchestra. In fact, they are always the ones asked to tour the United States." I admitted I hadn't heard them, but that I knew they appeared at Carnegie Hall.

A pause, then he asked (quite aggressively): "So tell me, there are at least 150,000 people out there. Is this the biggest crowd you have ever played for?"

"Well, sir," I said, "I did play with Diana Ross in New York's Central Park five years ago."

He, more aggressively: "Oh? And how many people were there?"

"Um, about 450,000," I replied.

The man literally deflated in front of my eyes . . . "H-h-ow you get that many in one place?," he sputtered.

I smiled and shrugged: "Well, sir, Central Park is pretty big . . ." He stalked off, leaving me almost feeling bad for bursting his balloon . . .

As for the concert itself, I wouldn't want to say that it was no different from any other—but ALL of Bruce's concerts were special in their way. His philosophy was this: "We're gonna work our asses off, but we're gonna have a great time doing it." The man puts out so much energy and commitment that one, as a "sideman," can't help but try to match it. I'm more a jazz guy than a rock 'n' roller, but there were plenty of nights were I physically reached what for me would be "wild abandon." And this one was no different. Just total concentration on what we were doing—so that we could follow and match whatever spontaneous direction Bruce would lead us in.

One thing I do recall vividly but probably so does the entire crowd: the girl that Bruce invited onstage to dance with him during *Dancing in the Dark*, which is a tradition of his. If you've seen the segment on YouTube, you'll understand that what crossed my mind was "If she's not careful, she's going to fall right out of that tanktop!" The only other trivial thing I almost guiltily remember is that as the concert ended, I saw the famed East German ice skater Katarina Witt make her way down the steps leading from the side of the stage. The last step to the ground was a big one. She hesitated for an instant. I put out my hand. She took it, smiled, and made the last step . . .

As we got ready to board the bus back to the hotel, we were told of being invited to a reception at the Communist Youth League headquarters, and it was hoped we would all go. But first we could take a little time to shower and change. As we walked back through the lobby, there was still a crowd. But they were all sitting—some were sleeping. And it was dead quiet. A disturbing thought occurred to me—were these all people who had planned to stay there but were "bumped" out of their rooms so we could have them? And now had nowhere else to go? Frankly, it bothered me. I felt guilty for having contributed to causing this . . .

After a shower and a change we reboarded the bus and rode through the pitch-black streets of East Berlin. We came to a medium-sized older brick building with lights ablaze. It was pleasant enough, but I didn't mingle all that much. I just stood outside for a bit, sipping on some wine and looking in. At one point, a number of officials started posing with Bruce for photographers. I felt a tug on my sleeve. It was Gert's girlfriend. She nodded towards the posing officials with Bruce, an almost-scowl on her face. "Not . . . good," she finally said.

"Oh?" I replied. Knowing I didn't understand, she motioned Gert over to us. An annoyed-sounding torrent of German went into Gert's ear. He nodded, then turned to me with a smile. "She wants to tell you that these government bigwigs don't even know who Bruce Springsteen is, and couldn't even care less about him. They just want their pictures taken with him to impress the young people . . ."

I smiled back. "Gert, tell her that it's absolutely no different in America. . . ."

We were still standing together when one official began a toast. "We thank Bruce Springsteen for providing the Deutsche Democratic Republic to now make three great W's in rock and roll history—Woodstock, Wembley, und Weisensee!"

I had to stifle any laughter on my part . . . We spent an hour or two there, then returned to the hotel, where there were no longer any people in the lobby. Not a single soul . . .

The next day we went over to West Berlin to play a concert at Waldbuehne on the 22. Going from a dull gray East Berlin to a brightly lit and lively West Berlin left me frankly feeling that reunification would be very hard, if not impossible. There was just too stark a difference between the two halves of the country.

But I was wrong.

In November 1989, just 16 months later, I was at a girlfriend's house. The Tunnel Tour was behind me, I had bought a house in East Orange, NJ, and was looking for gigs to play. I had a shortwave receiver so I was aware from listening to outlets such as the BBC, Deutsche Welle, and even Radio Berlin International that there were upheavals happening in the Eastern bloc. After dinner, I wandered into her living room. What's on TV? Wait a minute—what on earth is this??? Masses of people crowding the Wall. Joyously whacking away at it with hammers, crowbars, any heavy object at hand and then passing it to others to do the same. Sections of it just collapsing. I was glued to the TV—but also pacing back and forth. She couldn't quite get my excitement.

"You don't understand," I said, "I was there! I SAW that f----n' Wall close up and personal. And there's a big part of me that wishes I were with those folks right now! And maybe . . . just maybe . . . that concert I played with Bruce in a small way helped lead to this!"

Above: The press pass of our photographer, Herbert Schulze
Below: Conny Rudat's backstage pass and sticker.

Introduction

You can't start a fire without a spark
　　　　　–Dancing In the Dark

Bruce Springsteen was backstage, getting ready for what was the biggest and probably most eagerly awaited concert of his life. It was the summer of 1988, and he was at the height of his career. The thirty-eight-year-old rock star was cooped up in a temporary dressing room behind the makeshift stage in Communist East Berlin, on a vast open field, a former racetrack, that was quickly filling with hundreds of thousands of East Germans. Springsteen was in the midst of his "Tunnel of Love Express Tour" across Europe that summer and was elated to have the chance to take a quick detour across the Iron Curtain for an extra show in East Berlin.

It had only just been added to the summer schedule a few weeks earlier and it would be his only concert ever behind the Wall that divided Berlin, Germany, and Europe during the Cold War. The air was full of excitement in East Germany, in anticipation of the concert by this major Western rock star, whose songs about escape and the downtrodden had long been a source of inspiration. Springsteen may have had his home state of New Jersey on his mind when he wrote his soaring rock ballads, but his message of hope was universal. It had touched a nerve deep inside East Germany, formally known as the German Democratic Republic (Deutsche Demokratische Republik), a country sometimes known by its initials as the GDR, that locked up its seventeen million people behind an impermeable 12-foot-high concrete Wall.

Despite the bright mood and exuberant atmosphere as the concert approached on that balmy summer evening of July 19, 1988, there was a bit of tension backstage. A massive crowd of at least 300,000 East Germans, maybe even half a million according to some estimates, waited in the giant open-air venue about three miles east of the Berlin Wall. There had been such a crushing demand at the gates that the East German organizers eventually just threw open the security fences and let everyone in—a remarkable act of capitulation in the tightly controlled totalitarian state, and an eerie foreshadowing of what would happen to the Berlin Wall sixteen months later. Many in the crowd were already in a state of ecstasy—it was still hard for them to fathom that the man the world knew as "the Boss" had journeyed to their isolated country behind the Iron Curtain and that, for a few special hours, he would give them a tantalizing taste of the free world that was just beyond their reach, even though it was only a few miles away.

For his part, Springsteen had long wanted to give an East German audience the chance to see his style of an American rock 'n' roll concert—four hours of non-stop energy. He had gotten his first unforgettable glimpse of the Communist world on a trip across the Iron Curtain to East Berlin in 1981, as an ordinary tourist, and he had been eager to play for the people in East Germany ever since.

But even after he finally got permission to perform in East Berlin in 1988, the concert was suddenly in jeopardy the day before the show. After arriving in East Berlin, Springsteen and his manager found out that the East German concert organizers had put a "Concert for Nicaragua" spin on the event—a ruse to sell their Communist superiors on allowing this appearance by an American artist, a representative of the Eastern Bloc's arch enemy in the Cold War. During the 1980s, Nicaragua had become a rallying cry for the leftist cause, not only in the GDR, but around the world, because the CIA had backed efforts there to overthrow the left-wing Sandinistas during Ronald Reagan's presidency. But Springsteen was not going to lend his name to that cause. To Springsteen, the Nicaragua concert label was a provocative act of Cold War politics that would have implied an allegiance to the Socialist cause. And no matter how much empathy he may or may not have had for left-leaning causes or how much he may or may not have disliked Reagan, Springsteen had an aversion to his name being co-opted for political or commercial purposes.

The political move had upset Jon Landau—Springsteen's man-

Introduction

ager, adviser, sounding board, and close friend of many years. The idea of Springsteen doing a show for Nicaragua in East Germany was simply unacceptable. "It was an exploitation of his name and a misrepresentation of why he was there," Landau says today, still aghast, even twenty-five years later, by the audacity of the East German Communists. There was no way that Springsteen was going to do a benefit concert for Nicaragua on a stage draped with Communist propaganda.

East German officials feared the concert might be cancelled, a nightmare averted thanks to some quick work behind the scenes to remove most of the pro-Nicaragua banners and labels. But Springsteen was also determined to say a few words during the concert, to set the record straight on why he'd really wanted to do a show in East Berlin. Just before making his way to the stage, he summoned his translator, Georg Kerwinski, a jovial man from Bavaria who doubled as his chauffeur, for some help with his speech. No one, except Landau, knew what Springsteen was planning to tell the people of East Germany.

Backstage, Kerwinski came up with a German translation of the lines Springsteen told him he wanted to say. Springsteen thanked the cheerful German and was quickly out the door. He scampered up a narrow ramp onto the stage—to the deafening roar of the biggest crowd he had ever played before, a sea of smiling faces spread out across a vast park the size of fifty football fields, in the Weissensee district of East Berlin.

Springsteen got his concert off to a fast start with a rip-roaring rendition of *Badlands*, about an angry man yearning for a better life—a message quite possibly directed at the East German rulers. The mood was exuberant, there was magic in the air. Even the normally phlegmatic East German soldiers and security officers assigned to maintain a semblance of order at the venue could hardly contain their glee as the show hit full swing. Yet there was an anxious atmosphere backstage. Kerwinski had begun to wonder aloud about the wisdom of what he had just done—secretly helped an American draft a speech in German that might end up causing trouble for a lot of people.

The Bavarian chauffeur had a tremendous affinity for Springsteen, but his first loyalty was to his employer. So Kerwinski mentioned the looming speech to concert promoter Marcel Avram. The West German organizer was aghast and made a beeline for Landau, urging him to stop Springsteen from uttering the words to the East Berlin crowd that could doom them all. As the concert was already well into its second hour by then, Landau knew he had to act quickly. No one knew exactly when Springsteen planned to get the message off his chest. Landau waved his arms to catch Springsteen's attention on the stage and signaled for him to come down a set of stairs at the middle of the stage; Landau brought Kerwinski to meet him.

The band played on up above them while Springsteen huddled beneath the stage with Landau and Kerwinski. Landau told Springsteen they needed to make a small change. Shouting at the top of his lungs, Kerwinski tried to teach Springsteen the new word phonetically. They could barely hear each other. But after a moment Springsteen understood the message. He flashed a smile and gave Kerwinski a thumbs-up before climbing back up on stage. Only a few minutes later, right after singing an enthusiastic rendition of *Born in the USA*, Springsteen stepped back up to the microphone, looked out at the crowd, and then delivered what was probably the most powerful appeal for freedom anyone ever made inside East Germany.

This is the story about that speech and a rock concert that would change the world.

Chapter 1
The Year of Upheaval

I was a serious young man, you know?
 —Bruce Springsteen

Bruce Springsteen was one of the world's biggest rock stars in the summer of 1988. It was just four years after his most successful album, *Born in the USA*. The album made Springsteen and his music recognizable around the world, but he didn't always seem entirely comfortable with all of that stardom. 1988 was also three years after he got married to Julianne Phillips, an actress and fashion model. Problems at home were spilling out into the public that year, one that turned out to be full of change both professionally and personally. As he neared the age of forty, Springsteen was coming to another crossroads in his life. A decade earlier, as he approached thirty, he had seemed to be uncomfortable about aging. Back then he had talked about how the 1960s-era slogan "Don't trust anyone over thirty" weighed on his mind ahead of that milestone birthday. And now, ten years later, as the midlife threshold of forty loomed, Springsteen was looking for new directions, both in his music and in his personal life. The "Love Tunnel Express" album and tour was clearly a departure from his earlier work.

By 1988, Springsteen and his E Street Band had been together for sixteen years. After modest success in the early 1970s, they had soared to national prominence with the album *Born to Run* in 1975. After that came *Darkness on the Edge of Town* in 1978, before Springsteen and his band rocketed to international renown with *The River* in 1980, *Nebraska* in 1982 and *Born in the USA* in 1984. Springsteen and his E Street band had become one of the most sought-after acts on the planet, able to quickly sell out almost any indoor arena or outdoor stadium anywhere in the world, whenever and wherever they played.

Despite the growing fame and global glory, Springsteen was far from complacent in 1988, but in the midst of his own personal rebellion, a period of Sturm und Drang. By the mid-1980s, he was a major celebrity with huge audiences and mass followings in dozens of countries, thanks to *Born in the USA* and the accompanying world tour, with 156 stops in eleven countries on four continents, between June 1984, and October 1985. Five million people saw live Springsteen concerts during those grueling sixteen months on the road, and the tour generated $100 million in revenue. *Born in the USA* was one of the best-selling albums of all time, with twenty million copies sold. With a new sound more oriented to pop music and radio, it brought him into the lives of new fans all around the world, to regions far beyond the earlier bastions on the East Coast and pockets in the Midwest and South. Seven of the songs on the *Born in the USA* album were top-ten-chart hits in the United States.

Yet Springsteen was eager to experiment after *Born in the USA*. "There was a point in the mid-eighties when I felt like I'd said pretty much all I knew how to say about that . . . my experience growing up, my father's experience, the experience of my immediate family and town," he said in a 1998 interview with *Double Take* magazine. "There was a point in the mid-eighties where I wanted to turn my music into some kind of activity and action, so that there was a practical impact on communities that I passed through." He also wrote about his desire to try something new with the *Tunnel of Love* album, which included the popular songs *Two Faces, Tunnel of Love,* and *Brilliant Disguise*. "After '85 I'd had enough and turned inward to write about men, women, and love, things that previously had been on the periphery of my work," he said. *Tunnel of Love* was a departure—it did not include any of the rock-anthem-type of songs he and his E Street Band had delivered on *Born in the USA*. Much of *Tunnel of Love* explored the darker sides of relationships. Music critics called the album a sedate reflection on relationships—quite possibly on his own crumbling marriage. It ended up selling a respectable five million copies, but to

The Year of Upheaval

the bean-counters in the music industry that paled in comparison to his previous album.

But Springsteen did not seem bothered about that as he set off on a world tour in early 1988. The "Tunnel of Love Express Tour" took him to places like Philadelphia, Pittsburgh, Atlanta, Detroit, Los Angeles, and New York before he arrived in Europe in May. The "Express" in the title meant that the concerts were planned to last less than three hours, shorter than his usual four-hour gigs. The album included one of his most enduring ballads, *Brilliant Disguise,* about a man who is unsure of his own and his wife's faithfulness, with intriguing lyrics such as "I walk this world in wealth, I want to know if it's you I don't trust, 'cause I damn sure don't trust myself."

Springsteen's relationship with his band was going through a transformation at that time as well. The E Street Band had been an integral part of Springsteen's music and success since 1972. Yet the band was initially not involved at all with the recording of *Tunnel of Love.* Springsteen had worked on the album largely by himself, with the help of a drum machine and a synthesizer. He first recorded it alone and only later invited just a few E Street Band members to dub in their parts—Max Weinberg on drums, Roy Bittan on piano, and Danny Federici on organ. He had even contemplated doing the "Tunnel of Love Express Tour" solo, but scrapped that idea. The 1988 tour, though, would be the last time the E Street Band performed together with Springsteen for more than a decade. He formally broke up the E Street Band in October 1988, just a few months after the East Berlin concert. It was a devastating blow for some of the band members, as well as for millions of fans around the world. The E Street Band would not get back together for good until their "Reunion Tour" of 1999–2000.

Earlier in his career, before *Born in the USA,* Springsteen had resisted playing larger venues, worried about the loss of intimacy and diminished power of his music that might be the price to pay for playing in vast arenas. But each step up the ladder—from New Jersey nightclubs to smaller indoor arenas, to larger indoor arenas and outdoor stadiums—had turned out better than he had expected, in part because he worked hard at making sure every occupant of every seat was getting his or her money's worth, and also thanks to improvements in technology and sound equipment. Yet commercial success never seemed to be a major motivating factor for Springsteen—making music and moving people were the forces that drove him on. By the middle of 1988, he seemed at times to be longing for the more innocent and anonymous bar-band days of his earlier career. He also appeared to be ambivalent about his growing wealth and commercial clout. In 1988, four years after *Born in the USA* and a little more than a year before turning forty, Springsteen was, like the people in East Germany, ready for change.

There was trouble for Springsteen at home. His marriage wasn't working anymore and would end in divorce a few months later. The public disintegration of his marriage in the middle of 1988 was one of the few times in Springsteen's career when paparazzi pictures and stories about his private life provided fodder for gossip magazines. Springsteen and back-up singer Patti Scialfa became an item that summer. Until then, the general public knew relatively little about Springsteen's life off stage, in part because he worked to keep it private, and also because there had not been all that much to report on until then. Unlike many rock stars and other celebrities who ended up with problems associated with fame and fortune, Springsteen had been a rare exception and virtually scandal-free before 1988. An abstemious man who avoided alcohol and abhorred drugs, Springsteen did everything he could to prevent his growing celebrity from changing him. There were plenty of cautionary tales about the demise of those who did indulge, from his early idol Elvis Presley, to more than a few of his contemporaries. Springsteen also tried to shield his private life—only rarely giving interviews and preferring to let his songs and onstage performances do the talking for him.

Springsteen was always different from other rock stars. He might not have flourished at school, spending more time during his high school years with his guitar than studying his books and then later leaving Ocean County Community College in New Jersey without a degree. But he started reading novels and writing poetry in college and had an insatiable appetite for learning. In the two decades since the abrupt end of his formal education he had become a thoughtful, well read, widely traveled, and knowledgeable authority on a variety of issues, especially social history.

"I never did good in school, and they always figured that if you're not smart in school, it's because you're dumb," Springsteen said in a short speech between songs at a concert in Tempe, Arizona, in 1980—the night after Ronald Reagan was elected President. "But I always felt I never really learned anything, or learned anything that was important to me, till I started listening to the radio back in the early '60s." Springsteen said he learned a lot more from the music than he did at school. "They always talked to your head, they could never figure out how to talk to your heart, you know?" Later in that concert, Springsteen made his first public comments about politics, when he said that Reagan's election was frightening.

Springsteen stands five feet, nine inches tall and still had the same waist size at thirty-eight, when he played in East Berlin, that he'd had as an eighteen-year-old. He might not have talked as much about politics in 1988 as he would later in his career, but he was well on his way to becoming an outspoken artist-activist, sometimes ruminating on social and political issues to audiences between songs at concerts. By the late 1980s, with his political leanings unapologetically toward the left, Springsteen was becoming a voice for the proverbial "little guy." After the "Tunnel of Love Express Tour" wound down in August in Barcelona, just six stops after the concert in East Berlin, Springsteen joined the "Human Rights Now!" tour on behalf of Amnesty International, part of the celebrations to mark the fortieth anniversary of the Universal Declaration of Human Rights.

In 1988, Springsteen's music was stirring people from Tallahassee to Tokyo and from East Rutherford to East Berlin. But it was changing. Springsteen was a millionaire, thanks to *Born in the USA*, even if he still preferred to see himself as an ordinary troubadour with blue-collar roots and a working-class view of the world. Yet all along he believed that he was doing something important, more essential than just writing and playing music. He worked hard to make his music meaningful. Years later, in a famous 1996 interview with *The Advocate*, an American gay and lesbian news magazine, he reflected back on what he saw as the forces behind his music—the powers, for example, that had been strong enough to shake and rattle the younger generations of Communist East Germany. "I was a serious young man, you know?" Springsteen said, "I had serious ideas about rock music. Yeah it was also a circus and fun and a dance party—all of those things—but still a serious thing. I believed that serious things could be done with it. It had a power; it had a voice. I still fucking believe that. I really do."

On the road, Springsteen was a passionate observer, in particular on his European tours. He soaked up the different cultures and languages, going out of his way to learn pithy phrases in the native tongue to sprinkle in a few French or Spanish or German lines into his monologues with the audience between songs. Springsteen has often said he had a desire to make rock 'n' roll relevant to people, regardless of their age, income, race, religion or nationality. In the 1998 *Double Take* interview he also said, "I had some lofty ideas about using my own music, to give people something to think about—to think about the world, and what's right and wrong." In a rare but lengthy television interview with Ted Koppel for the ABC network in 2002, Springsteen opened up a bit and talked about his desire to make a difference—he may well have had concerts like East Berlin in 1988 in mind. "I wanted to do work that had an impact and was relevant and addressed the ideas of the day and what I thought was important," Springsteen said.

The surge of popularity that turned Springsteen into an international celebrity in 1984, at the height of the *Born in the USA* craze, was summarized in a splendid four-minute national television news report by Bernhard Goldberg of CBS Nightly News on September 12, 1984: "Springsteen sings about Americans, blue-collar Americans trapped and suffocating in old broken-down small towns. His songs are about working-class people, desperate people hanging on to the American dream by a thread. His songs may be about disillusionment, but the energy tells you the message is hope. Bruce Springsteen is the American dream—his roots are blue-collar New Jersey. His father was a bus driver, often out of work. The message is: work hard and you'll succeed."

Goldberg knew his subject well and understood the essence of Springsteen. "He sings about the contradictions of freedom and powerlessness in America, about teenagers who still dream and about adults who know how things really end up . . . He touches his fans and they touch him," Goldberg concluded, as a film clip showed a pack of frenzied women jumping up and over a line of security guards and onto the stage to hug Springsteen, who did little to resist the onslaught of female admirers and is last seen smiling as he falls onto his back and disappears under a pile of ecstatic women.

What did Springsteen want to accomplish with his music? He was asked that straightforward question in another interview in 1984, on the MTV music video network. His answer was as simple as it was memorable: "The only message, really, is don't sell yourself short, ya know?" In East Germany in 1988, that was exactly the message that a young and restless generation got.

Despite the changes in his own life in 1988, Springsteen was still going all out to give audiences on the "Tunnel of Love Express Tour" a show worth what he himself often referred to as their hard-earned money. Yet to those who followed Springsteen's concert tours throughout the 1980s, the "Tunnel of Love Express Tour" that began in Worcester, Massachusetts, on February 28, 1988, was different, as Springsteen biographer Dave Marsh noted in his book *Two Hearts: Bruce Springsteen, the Definitive Biography, 1975–2003*. Springsteen seemed pleased to move away from the mass audiences that packed cavernous stadiums during the "Born in the USA Tour."

During the first part of the "Tunnel of Love Express Tour," in the United States from February to May 1988, he was playing in smaller indoor arenas again. Marsh said that Springsteen had "established a creative oscillation of sorts, between mass appeal projects and more personal, 'artier' ones, a balance unlike any other superstar's. This was important for reasons of image and sanity, but it counted for nothing at record stores, which cared only for tonnage." Marsh said Springsteen's *Tunnel of Love* was considered a disappointment by the star-making machinery he was a part of in 1988. But Springsteen didn't seem to care about that. "Rather than returning to outdoor stadiums, he went back to the indoor arenas that had sustained him for the decade before," Marsh observed. "But at least initially, the tour departed in startling ways from the previous E Street Band extravaganzas: it was somewhat shorter and many of the seemingly irreplaceable warhorse concert pieces, even such landmarks as 'Badlands,' 'Thunder Road,' and 'The Promised Land' were discarded . . . This was a great show because it challenged the perceptions and expectations of Springsteen fans—not just the mass audience that had first been reached by 'Born in the USA' . . . Soon enough the shows were back up to four hours."

In the summer of 1988, Springsteen was back in Europe, where he has always been welcomed with open arms. He was playing in larger outdoor stadiums again, beginning in Turin on June 13, and then he traveled on to Rome, Paris, Birmingham, London, Rotterdam, Stockholm, Dublin, Sheffield, Frankfurt, Basel, and Munich before adding the stop in East Berlin. On the "Tunnel of Love Express Tour," Springsteen played songs from the new album, as well as many of his earlier hits, during concerts that started in broad daylight in the long European summer evenings and lasted well into the darkness some three to four hours later.

Springsteen wasn't able to keep the turmoil in his private life entirely out of the public eye during the European leg of the "Tunnel of Love Express Tour." His wife's publicist had announced their separation in June. Springsteen had little to say about the changes at the time, but later, in a 1997 interview with *The New York Times Magazine*, he reflected on his marriage to Julianne Phillips. He said they had simply grown apart. "We were pretty different, and I realized I didn't know how to be married," Springsteen said.

But in July and August 1988, tabloid newspapers across Europe were printing pictures of Springsteen together with Patti Scialfa. She had joined the band as a background vocalist in 1984, after Springsteen felt the band had become too much of a "boys club." Like Springsteen, she was from New Jersey, from a town only a few miles away from his hometown of Freehold. By the time the "Tunnel of Love Express Tour" arrived in East

Berlin, their romance was in full bloom, both on and off the stage. Just six weeks after the East Berlin concert, on August 30, Springsteen and Phillips filed for divorce, and Bruce was ready to start a new chapter in his life.

East German fans holding up a hand-made American flag.
Photo: Herbert Schulze

The famous border crossing sign at Checkpoint Charlie in West Berlin. Below: A section of the Wall from the West Berlin side in the district of Kreuzberg in 1988.

Chapter 2
HE HAD A DREAM

Baby this town rips the bones from your back
It's a death trap, it's a suicide rap
We gotta get out while we're young
'cause tramps like us, baby we were born to run
—Born to Run

At the same time that Springsteen's life was going through a period of upheaval in 1988, there were also undercurrents of change rippling across Europe. The Cold War was speeding toward an unexpected and abrupt conclusion that few saw coming. The frosty post–World War II standoff between the United States–led Western nations and the Soviet Union–led Eastern Bloc countries would wind down less than a year and a half later. Revolutionary changes in Europe gained momentum with increasingly bold protests in Poland, Hungary, and East Germany in 1989, which led first to the collapse of the GDR's hard-line Communist dictatorship and the climactic breaching of the Berlin Wall. The most powerful uprising since the end of World War II then rolled further across the rest of Eastern Europe, toppling one Communist regime after another in quick succession.

But in mid-1988, Europe was still coldly divided between the Communist Bloc and the Capitalist West when Springsteen and his band journeyed merrily across the western half of the continent on his "Tunnel of Love Express Tour." When the sixty-six stop "Tunnel of Love Express Tour" was announced on January 6, 1988, there was no East Berlin concert date on the calendar, nor any show anywhere else in Communist Eastern Europe. For the Western European leg of the tour that summer, there were twenty-five concerts scheduled, starting on June 11 in Turin, Italy, and concluding on August 3 in Barcelona, Spain, with stops in between in France, England, the Netherlands, Sweden, Ireland, Switzerland, West Germany, Denmark, and Norway. It was in the midst of this two-month European tour that Springsteen announced at a stop in Stockholm on July 3 that he had signed up to join the "Human Rights Now!" tour on behalf of Amnesty International—a tour of benefit concerts scheduled for later in the year with Sting, Peter Gabriel, and Tracy Chapman. It would be a six-week, twenty-stop tour to celebrate the fortieth anniversary of the Universal Declaration of Human Rights and raise awareness about it.

Springsteen was no stranger to awareness-raising musical efforts. He had taken part in the 1985 "We Are the World" charity single for African famine relief. Before that, he had been a significant and influential supporter of the Vietnam Veterans of America Foundation and taken part in the 1979 anti-nuclear "Musicians United for Safe Energy" (MUSE) concert. Around the same time that he signed up for the human rights tour in 1988, Springsteen was wondering about the prospects of doing a show in East Berlin that summer, too. Playing in East Berlin, after all, had been on Springsteen's mind for years. So Springsteen turned to his manager, Jon Landau.

Landau, a bespectacled man with thinning hair who is two years older than Springsteen, is a rock music critic, manager, and producer par excellence. He has been Springsteen's go-to guy since 1975. After seeing him play in a small club in 1974, Landau wrote arguably one of the most famous rock music reviews of all time, for a Boston alternative weekly called *The Real Paper*, in which he stated: "I saw rock and roll future and its name is Bruce Springsteen." Landau has also been a critic for *Rolling Stone*. At first he only co-produced Springsteen's albums, but later took on the role of manager as well. He is widely credited with having a major influence on Springsteen, both intellectually and artistically, and the two have always been close. Springsteen gave Landau the chance to fulfill a lifelong dream of being in a rock band, by letting him sit in on a series of concerts about a decade ago. Landau lost sight in one eye in 2011, resulting from surgery to have a growth removed. Springsteen spent nearly every day with Landau for a while after that.

He Had a Dream

Landau clearly remembers Springsteen's enduring interest in going to East Berlin. "Bruce came up to me and asked 'What are the chances of working a show into East Berlin?' I told him I'd check. So we approached our regular West German promoter, Marcel Avram, and asked him if he had any experience in East Germany. And he did. So he made all the arrangements. There was a lot going on that summer, with the anniversary of the Declaration of Human Rights from 1948, so we had those kinds of issues in our minds. With all the talk of the Amnesty International tour coming up later that year, Bruce just thought it would be a timely thing to do. The principle thing is that we wanted to play East Berlin at that point. Bruce really wanted to go to East Berlin."

The week after Stockholm, Springsteen played in Frankfurt on July 12, then in Basel, Switzerland, on July 14, and in Munich on the 17th. He had a five-day break before the next scheduled concert on July 22, in West Berlin. There was an opening there, Landau remembers. The response from East Germany this time was unexpectedly positive, as Springsteen later told the East German DDR2 television network during an intermission in his July 1988 concert. "We were very excited when we called and the response was immediate," Springsteen said. "It was like 'Yes, come on over.'"

Springsteen's ambition to do a concert in East Germany can be traced at least as far back as 1981, when he crossed over the Berlin Wall into East Berlin as an ordinary tourist on a one-day visa. Like many Americans who went behind the Iron Curtain into East Berlin, he was fascinated by the Communist half of the city and by the people living behind the Berlin Wall that had physically cut the already politically divided city in half since 1961. He would have done a concert in East Berlin in 1981 if he could have. But there was a period of deep chill in the Cold War in the early 1980s, and hell would have to freeze over before the East German authorities would allow a Western rock star to perform on their territory back then. Yet seven years later, by the middle of 1988, the winds were shifting in many countries across Eastern Europe. The disdain toward Western rock music and the ban on concerts by Western acts was lifting, thanks in part to *glasnost* (openness) and *perestroika* (restructuring)—economic and government reforms introduced in 1985 by new Soviet leader Mikhail Gorbachev. Attitudes were changing in East Germany as well, in part because the Communist rulers began to realize that the younger generations were increasingly turned off by the Communist system and turning away from the Socialist ideals at an alarming rate.

Before Gorbachev's epoch-making reforms, the Soviet satellite states across Eastern Europe were controlled by Moscow—a policy that had been known since 1968 as the Brezhnev Doctrine, named after Soviet ruler Leonid Brezhnev, who died in 1982. The policy's underlying notion was that if one Socialist country were to turn toward Capitalism, it would present a common problem to all Socialist countries. The argument was used to justify Soviet crackdowns on an ephemeral liberalization movement in Czechoslovakia in 1968, when Soviet tanks rolled in to put down the uprising. Similar short-lived rebellions in the Baltic region throughout the 1950s, East Germany in 1953, and Hungary in 1956 were crushed equally as swiftly with the same justification. Just a year after the Springsteen concert in East Berlin, the Brezhnev Doctrine would be replaced by what was facetiously called the "Sinatra Doctrine"—each country going its own way—a wry allusion to Frank Sinatra's song "My Way," coined by a Soviet foreign ministry official in October 1989. It was seen as the Soviet Union releasing its Eastern Bloc allies to decide their own destinies for themselves. East Germany's hard-line ruler, Erich Honecker, was unnerved about the threat that the Gorbachev reforms represented to his control.

A short, stern man with gray hair and a high, squeaky voice, Honecker was seventy-five years old in 1988. He was isolated from ordinary East Germans and an increasingly solitary figure. Born in 1912 in a southwestern German state called the Saarland, Honecker joined the Communist Party at the age of twenty-eight. In 1935, shortly after the Nazis came to power, he was arrested by the Gestapo and spent ten years in a Berlin prison, until the Soviet Red Army freed him near the end of World War II. He was one of the founders of the GDR, together with Walter Ulbricht, and was in charge of the Communist youth organization called the Freie Deutsche Jugend (Free German Youth), or FDJ as it was commonly known. Honecker rose in status after overseeing the construction of the Berlin Wall in 1961. He took over leadership of the Sozialistische Einheitspartei Deutschlands (Socialist Unity Party; SED), more commonly known as the East German Communist Party, in 1971, and ruled the country for nearly two decades. He was a staunch critic of Gorbachev's reforms and warned that they would destroy Socialist unity in the Soviet Bloc.

Under Honecker's leadership in the late 1980s, East Germany had one of the last remaining hard-line Communist regimes—in an orbit with countries like Romania and Cuba. And unlike other Eastern European countries, such as Poland, Hungary, and Czechoslovakia, that were gradually opening up under the *glasnost* and *perestroika* reforms, the East German government resisted those changes. East German border guards were still shooting and killing people who tried to flee the country to the West. The East German security apparatus was still working intensively and effectively to suppress any dissident movements. Stifled younger generations in East Germany were increasingly fed up with the stagnant state of affairs. By the summer of 1988, many young East Germans were ready for change. They watched with envy as the Gorbachev-inspired reforms spread throughout other Socialist Eastern European countries but made an exasperating detour around their own.

When Springsteen had been in East Berlin before, during his quiet, private visit as a tourist in April 1981, it was a darker time during the Cold War and just a few months after Ronald Reagan was inaugurated as America's fortieth President. It was also four years before Mikhail Gorbachev took power in the Soviet Union and introduced his *perestroika* and *glasnost* reforms.

1981 was also well before the *Born in the USA* album and tour that would turn Springsteen into a global celebrity. He was just starting out on his first full concert run through Western Europe with "The River Tour." There were thirty-four concerts scheduled during the three-month European leg of "The River Tour." The first was in Hamburg on April 7, which turned into an improbable success when the normally stoic Northern Germans jumped out of their seats to dance to his music after an initially chilly reception.

Springsteen then traveled from Hamburg across about 180 miles of Communist East Germany to the Capitalist island of West Berlin, for a concert at the International Congress Center (ICC) on the next evening, April 8. It was a pleasant Wednesday in early spring, with afternoon temperatures rising up to the mid-fifties. The ICC was a 5,000-seat indoor venue inside a modern, silver metallic building that locals sometimes joked looked more like a spaceship than a concert hall. Perched on a hill overlooking West Berlin, about five miles away from Berlin's city center, the convention center had opened just two years earlier, in 1979. It was Springsteen's first-ever performance in West Berlin.

He and his E Street Band had a three-day break before their next concert in Zurich, Switzerland, on Saturday, April 11. They deliberately scheduled lots of extra free time between shows in Europe, so that everyone could have a chance to see the sights, talk to people, and learn more about Europe. "The River Tour" was an eye-opening experience for Springsteen and gave the thirty-one-year-old from New Jersey fresh insights about the world and the United States from a European perspective.

Americans traveling in Europe during the Reagan era were sometimes confronted with sharp questions from locals about U.S. government policies. It usually didn't take long for Europeans to start grilling Americans about U.S. Pershing II missiles, medium-range nuclear missiles based in West Germany and pointed at Eastern Bloc countries like East Germany, while Soviet SS-20 missiles based in East Germany were pointed in the opposite direction. Americans often discovered that West Germans and East Germans tended to know more about the United States and the intricacies of U.S. foreign policies than most Americans did. Springsteen and has band would have similar experiences. On the day after the West Berlin concert, Springsteen went over to the other side, like hundreds of other Western tourists did each day, across the Wall to East Berlin.

The East Berlin that Springsteen saw in 1981 was a dismal place—the bleak, gray rump of what had been Germany's biggest and most vibrant city from the "Golden Twenties" to World War II. Berlin was badly damaged by U.S. and British bombing raids during the war. Soviet artillery shelling and fierce street fighting at the end of the war had turned sections of the capital city into giant piles of rubble. In contrast to East Berlin—where the cash-strapped East German Communist Party (SED) had other priorities—West Berlin was a pulsating city of two million, with bright lights and bustling streets. A colorful island of Western-style democracy surrounded by Communist East Germany, West Berlin took on the role of freedom's most famous outpost and became a spy and media hub as well, for operations and broadcasts into Eastern Europe. For the Western Allies and West German government, it had been politically important to restore West Berlin as a glittering showcase for Capitalism, with luxurious hotels, well-stocked shops, and swanky bars and restaurants—at great expense to West German taxpayers who spent billions of marks every year to keep the city afloat.

There was probably no better place in the world than in Berlin to get a first-hand glimpse of the perils of the Cold War and a powerful feeling for the two rival systems. The striking differences, both tangible and intangible, between the Communist and the Capitalist worlds that faced off against each other on opposite sides of the Berlin Wall were part of daily life in West Berlin, whose freedom was zealously protected by ten thousand Allied soldiers—from the United States, Britain and France. Throughout the Cold War there was a lingering fear in West Berlin of being overrun by the Soviets and Warsaw Pact armies, which had more than 300,000 battle-ready troops based just outside West Berlin's borders. Subsequently, many West Berliners left and in their place came students, artists, draft-dodgers, and squatters from West Germany as well as Turkish immigrants.

Until the Wall was built in the middle of the night on August 13, 1961, East and West Berlin were geographically still one city, yet politically divided and straddling two worlds. Yet the people of those two worlds still had the same traditions, language, and culture. Many were even related—brothers, sisters, aunts, uncles, cousins, grandparents, in-laws, and distant relatives. Suddenly separated by the Wall in 1961, it wasn't until 1963 that West Berliners were allowed to visit their Eastern relatives again. The East German government built the Wall around West Berlin to stop a brain drain, because hundreds of thousands of the East's best and brightest were fleeing to better-paying jobs and greater freedoms in the West. East Germany's official stance, however, was that the Wall was an "antifascist protection barrier". Some in the West were sympathetic to its real function as an East-West barrier. When it was built, even U.S. President John F. Kennedy recognized that the Berlin Wall, no matter how ugly it was, had defused tensions in East Berlin. "A Wall is a hell of a lot better than a war," he said. During a television interview two weeks before the Wall was built, Kennedy adviser and Arkansas senator William Fulbright wondered out loud why East Germany hadn't built a wall yet. Harold Macmillan, British prime minister at the time, agreed that there was nothing illegal about stopping a stream of refugees.

Under Communist rule, East Berlin had developed into a dreary and fear-filled place, especially after the 1961 division. The East German Ministry for State Security (Ministerium für Staatssicherheit, or "Stasi"), kept tight control over the 1.3 million East Berliners and seventeen million East Germans. The German Democratic Republic was established in 1949 as a Socialist state based on an egalitarian society, founded mostly by Communist anti-Nazi resistance fighters who saw their new state as the righteous answer to the Third Reich—not surprisingly, since the GDR was occupied by the Soviets after the Allied victory in World War II and subsequent division of Germany, and was a puppet state of the Soviet Union.

In theory, the GDR was a workers' paradise, with the means of production nationalized in government-owned factories and massive subsidies for life's basic necessities. There was no unemployment, because everyone was obliged to contribute productive work and not be a "drain on society." Like Leipzig or Dresden, East Berlin was a ridiculously inexpensive city, with cheap food prices, subway tickets costing just a few cents, and government-owned, low-rent housing. Wage gaps were also small in the GDR, where most people, men and women alike, earned an average 1,300 Marks a month in East German currency, officially about $650. The East German government maintained that one East Mark was equal to one West Mark (about half a U.S. dollar), but the exchange rate for East Marks in the West was around 1:4 on the black market, where the East Mark had little value. With basic necessities so heavily subsidized, though, and items officially identified as luxuries harder to come by, money hardly mattered, and most had enough for an average standard of living. A popular underground slogan in East Germany aptly described the system and its myriad inefficiencies: "You pretend to pay us, and we'll pretend to work."

As in other Communist nations, things didn't quite work out as planned. To prevent or thwart any challenge to its lock on power, East Germany's totalitarian regime tightly controlled many aspects of people's lives and kept close tabs on anyone suspected of being an enemy of the state. Swift action was taken against any dissidents. Tens of thousands of people were imprisoned on trumped-up charges. Basic liberties, such as freedom to travel, freedom of assembly, a free press, and freedom of speech, were denied. There were also no free elections in East Germany. The Communist SED did not tolerate any political opposition.

The state also held complete control over the media, and the East German education system was laced with anti-Western and especially anti-American propaganda. Fearful of an anti-Communist uprising, East German authorities even imposed tight controls on the use of photocopy machines and telephones, lest a revolt spread from below. The state tried to control what people were allowed to say and where they were allowed to go. Travel for most East Germans was allowed only within the Eastern Bloc. Only a limited number of carefully selected elite athletes, scientists or trade representatives were allowed to travel to the West.

There were other prices to pay for the GDR's well-padded social net. With the state—rather than the marketplace—controlling how many shoes, toasters, or toothbrushes were manufactured or imported, there were shortages of just about everything, and "luxury" items like cars, color TVs, and cassette recorders were extremely expensive. East Germans also endured chronic shortages of popular imported items such as bananas and coffee beans, because the state was reluctant or unable to divert its short supply of convertible currency for imported tropical fruits or luxury goods.

East Berlin's wide boulevards were largely devoid of cars, and the few vehicles that puttered around were small, smelly contraptions that their owners had to wait years for after placing their orders.

The unflashy Trabant and Wartburg cars on East German roads were built using 1950s technology, and little effort was made to improve upon the early cramped and uncomfortable models. With their underpowered two-stroke engines, they were not the kind of cars that might have inspired Springsteen to write songs about.

East Berlin was also devoid of bright lights and advertising, except for the ubiquitous Communist battle cries printed in bright red letters, such as "DDR—Retter des Friedens" (The GDR—Savior of Peace) and "Der Sozialismus siegt" (Socialism Shall Triumph). Westerners on tour buses were known to have broken into spontaneous applause when crossing the border back to West Berlin, experiencing an instant rush of freedom as they left behind East Berlin and its dreary atmosphere of oppression and fear. The East-West border became a sinister prop in West Berlin's show for Western tourists, who could climb onto special platforms set up at the Wall and gaze over the barrier that split the city from 1961 to 1989.

They saw a gray and lifeless "death strip" down below, which ranged from a few dozen yards across to a few hundred yards wide as it wended its way through the heart of the city. Tourists often spotted East German border guards standing in their guard towers opposite them on the East Berlin side of the Wall, menacingly staring back at them through binoculars. It was a chilly confrontation, pure Cold War drama. The "death strip" between the Wall and the East Berlin guard towers was a flood-lit, no-man's land filled with sand pits and jeep patrol lanes, where people trying to escape could easily be spotted and, if they didn't stop running, shot.

Between 1961 and 1989, more than 100,000 East Germans tried to escape over or under the Berlin Wall or across the border between East Germany and West Germany. Some jumped out of open windows near the Wall, before those buildings were torn down and the Wall was fortified, while others climbed over the barbed wire, swam across rivers, or even crawled through the sewer system in their quest for freedom. Some built tunnels, while others flew over the Wall in homemade hot air balloons or ultralight airplanes, under cover of darkness. More than 1,000 were killed trying to get over the Wall or the German–German border. In Berlin, a total of 136 were killed while trying to escape.

He Had a Dream

The mere act of attempting to flee East Germany was considered a crime under the peculiar East German definition of justice. About 3,200 people were caught and sent to prison on charges of "Republikflucht" (fleeing the republic). Historians have counted more than 5,000 who made it successfully over, under, or through the Berlin Wall to freedom in West Berlin, during the twenty-eight years it divided the city in two.

Although the Berlin Wall was impermeable from the East, it was possible for Westerners with special visas to pass through in the other direction to the East, after 1963. Tourists and travelers from the West were allowed to cross over into East Berlin through fourteen tightly guarded "Checkpoints"—East-West gateways along the 100-mile border separating West Berlin from East Germany—including what was probably the most famous border crossing of all at "Checkpoint Charlie," provided they passed close inspection by East German border guards and paid the obligatory minimum daily exchange of twenty-five West German marks for twenty-five East German marks. The "Zwangsumtausch" or "forced exchange," as it was known, was another source of Western currency for the East German government, although the 1:1 exchange rate was hardly fair. But Westerners traveling to East Berlin had no choice. They had to buy the East German marks at the unfavorable rate and often struggled to find anything they wanted to buy with their East Marks. Border crossings were tense; anyone caught carrying anything in their bags as innocuous as a Western newspaper or magazine into East Germany, or anything else East German officials considered to be contraband Western propaganda, could be held up for hours at the checkpoints or even sent back to West Berlin without further explanation.

East Germans, by contrast, had no chance to cross the border freely to West Berlin, with or without an East German newspaper tucked into their pocket. They were in essence held captive in their own country, cut off from the bright lights and freedoms of West Berlin and Western Europe. An exception to the rules was granted to senior citizens. Rather cynically, East Germany let its retirees cross the border to West Germany, even with one-way tickets out, because after their working careers were finished they were seen as a burden to society. Allowing seniors to emigrate meant fewer retirees for the state pension and health care systems to worry about; East Germany was willing to shoot at anyone under sixty-five to keep them in, but had no qualms about exporting its no-longer-productive seniors to West Germany.

As a baby-boomer who grew up in the United States with the Cold War as the defining global struggle, Springsteen was curious to visit a place like Communist East Berlin. Taught to fear that nations could fall to Communism like dominos and haunted by the specter of a U.S.–Soviet nuclear showdown, Springsteen wanted to find out for himself what life was really like behind the Iron Curtain. He relished the chance to pass through the border crossing and meet locals in 1981. It was an illuminating visit, and it bothered him that the people in the eastern half of Berlin had no chance of seeing his concert in West Berlin. A seed was planted in Springsteen's mind: he wanted to play in East Berlin. "The next time we come to Berlin, everyone's going to be invited to the party," Springsteen told his manager, Landau.

It is not hard to imagine why East Germany had no interest in letting an American rock star perform in 1981. Cold War tensions between the United States and Soviet Union were worsening in the months after Ronald Reagan was inaugurated as President in January 1981. Less than a year earlier, the United States had led a boycott by many Western nations of the Moscow Olympic Games in 1980, after the Soviet Union invaded Afghanistan. In early 1981, the new American President was working to increase the number of the U.S. nuclear missiles in Western Europe pointed at East Germany and the Soviet Union—in response to a build-up of Soviet intermediate range nuclear missiles capable of hitting targets in West Germany and across Western Europe.

In 1981, aging hardliners were firmly ensconced in power in both Moscow and East Berlin. In the entire Soviet Bloc, the United States was viewed as the enemy and a threat to world peace. Americans were often portrayed as trigger-happy, imperialist aggressors itching to start World War III —a view shared by most leftists in the West. After Reagan was elected and the Cold War grew even colder, Germans both East and West were petrified by apocryphal stories such as U.S. travel agents using fear tactics to encourage Americans to book visits to Europe: "See Europe as long as it still exists."

Further complicating matters for any Western artist eager to play in East Germany was the fact that the ruling Communist Party had long tried to keep Western rock music out of the country. The official view was that it was a distraction from Socialism, a nefarious cultural weapon, and it would have a corrupting influence on young people. Jochen Staadt, a political historian at Berlin's Free University, said that the attempts to keep rock out were increasingly ineffective and abandoned in the 1970s, in large part because Western music was so popular and so widely available on West German, U.S., and British radio networks that were also deliberately beamed into East Germany. The Communists did, however, place strict controls on their own East German rock bands and their lyrics. East German bands had to obtain state-issued permits to play in public, and Western bands were only rarely allowed in for concerts—and then with onerous restrictions. Oddly enough, if East German authorities had taken a moment to listen more closely at Springsteen's music in 1981, they might have been more receptive.

Many of Springsteen's songs are about disillusionment and the darker sides of life in the United States, the disappointments, the dispossessed, and the hardships facing the working class, along with the emotional struggles of life in a country with such wide disparities of wealth. East German authorities and the state-run media had often focused on America's shortcomings—from high unemployment to homelessness in the land of unbridled capitalism, from its treatment of the poor and under-privileged to the proliferation of violent crime. Springsteen's father had a difficult time staying gainfully employed, working for a while in a rug mill and as a bus driver. His struggles to make ends meet are a well-documented part of Springsteen's life—which clearly had an influence on his songwriting. That was all lost, however, on East Germany in 1981. But in 1988, Springsteen advocates in East Germany's Communist FDJ youth organization emphasized those working-class credentials in their appeal to the higher-ups in the Communist Party to get approval for Springsteen to perform in East Berlin.

A poster of the Tunnel of Love *concert tour signed by Springsteen.*

Chapter 3
CHIMES OF FREEDOM

Badlands you gotta live it every day
Let the broken hearts stand
As the price you've gotta pay
We'll keep pushin' till it's understood
And these badlands start treating us good
                                                     —Badlands

By 1987 and 1988, the situation in East Germany and the entire Eastern Bloc was changing. Reforms launched by Soviet leader Mikhail Gorbachev in 1985, after Springsteen's first visit in 1981, were spreading across Eastern Europe, but there was resistance from East Germany's hardliners, who turned a deaf ear to any demands for change.

Many younger East Germans were growing fed up with the stifled atmosphere and lack of personal liberties. But what could they do about it? It was a toxic mixture of frustration and discontent, exacerbated by a suffocating sense of a growing economic disparity between the East and West. That worsening gap was made clear to East Germans through a steady stream of Western music and information beamed into their country from radio and television networks in West Berlin. With an area of 41,610 square miles, East Germany was about the same size as Kentucky, and radio broadcasts from West Germany could be heard across most of East Germany. Western radio and TV broadcasts played a similar role in spreading information to the masses in East Germany as the Internet's role three decades later in contributing to the Arab Spring uprisings in the Middle East in 2011.

Gorbachev's reforms of the mid-1980s were having a huge impact on parts of the Soviet Bloc. At fifty-four, Gorbachev was unusually young when he assumed the title of General Secretary of the Communist Party in 1985, after a succession of elderly Soviet rulers had died while in power. He first pushed his *perestroika* (restructuring) reform in the Soviet Union and later his *glasnost* (openness) efforts to try to end a period of economic stagnation and make the Socialist system more efficient at a time when it was falling further behind the West. The reforms were also designed to give Soviet satellite states across Eastern Europe more independence from Moscow. *Perestroika* and *glasnost* served as a catalyst for great changes in Eastern Europe which eventually led to the collapse of Communism and later the Soviet Union itself. In East Germany, however, hard-line, Stalinist-era leader Erich Honecker made little secret of his disdain for Gorbachev's reforms. He considered Gorbachev to be a dangerous charlatan who wouldn't last long, and he resisted, blocked, and largely ignored Moscow's call for reforms.

The people of East Germany, though, were cognizant of the way the winds were blowing and envious of the increasing freedoms in other Eastern European countries, particularly of the Solidarity movement in neighboring Poland. East Germans tracked Moscow's shifting attitudes and their effects in many ways. One of the more striking changes could be seen in the progressively bold content of the German-language edition of *Sputnik* magazine, a popular monthly digest of newspaper articles from the Soviet Union. After Gorbachev's arrival on the scene in the mid-1980s, *Sputnik* started printing attention-grabbing articles that challenged the standard Communist Party line and its often distorted views on post-war European history. East German readers were fascinated by this new openness and critical commentary from Moscow in such a seemingly official publication, and the mid-1980s saw an increase in the number of avid *Sputnik* readers in East Germany. But *Sputnik*'s challenge to the standard party line did not sit well with East German rulers. The digest became so critical that the East German government eventually banned its distribution in November 1988 on the grounds that it was "not contributing to German-Soviet friendship" and "distorting history"—less than four months after Springsteen played in East Berlin.

While it was just one more magazine joining a long list of Western publications prohibited in East Germany, this was a Soviet publication—from the powerful, long-time leader of the Eastern Bloc—and a chilling moment for many East Germans. There had long been fear among ordinary East Germans of how long the Gorbachev thaw might last, and in their eyes, banning *Sputnik* was a wrong step in the wrong direction.

Because the *perestroika* and *glasnost* reforms were having such a profound effect on East Germany's neighbors and other countries throughout Eastern Europe, there was a powerful yearning, especially among younger East Germans, to see some "restructuring" and "openness" start to take hold in their country as well. By 1988, the East German government was not going to make any significant concessions on any issues that really mattered but was beginning to reluctantly agree to some modest ideas to placate the youth, such as rock concerts organized by the Communist regime's official youth wing, the FDJ.

The mission of the FDJ (Freie Deutsche Jugend), which was created in 1949, was nominally to keep young people between the ages of fourteen and twenty-five supportive and enthused about Communism, the Socialist system, and East Germany. In theory, membership was voluntary, but those who did not join—mostly children from religious families—could forget about getting accepted to universities or face even more ominous consequences. In 1985, FDJ membership was at 2.3 million, or about eighty percent of all East Germans in the fourteen-to-twenty-five age bracket. The FDJ uniform included a long-sleeved blue shirt with a small, yellow "FDJ" patch on the left sleeve. At a minimum, the FDJ was supposed to work to prevent the younger generations from staging any sort of rebellion. In the late 1980s, the FDJ was fully aware that support for the country's Marxist-Leninist policies was waning while frustration among many East Germans was waxing. Attempting to keep young people at least somewhat content in 1988, the FDJ leadership proposed such things as putting on rock concerts with East German bands and inviting top Western artists to perform on an open lot in the Weissensee district. "The changes

Gorbachev had launched were met with skepticism by the East German rulers—they simply rejected them," says Roland Claus, a thirty-three-year-old FDJ leader at the time of the 1988 concert, whose once-amber hair has long since turned gray. Claus is now a Left Party member of the German parliament, the successor party to the former East German Communist Party (SED). "We were a group of younger leaders in the FDJ and tried to tell them that was the wrong way to go, that we had to open ourselves to the world. We knew we had to do something for the young people. We proposed holding concerts in East Berlin with international stars. That was something new."

Communist rulers had previously refused such an opening but grudgingly agreed in 1988, and granted approval for concerts by Western artists, which would have been unimaginable just a few years earlier. It was a belated attempt to pacify the increasingly restless masses. The East German regime's shifting attitude did not go unnoticed. The same Communist hardliners—young and old—who had rejected and disparaged Western rock music before were now welcoming Western rock stars into their capital. "It was a paradoxical situation," says Gerd Dietrich, a history professor at Berlin's Humboldt University. "Before Springsteen, the FDJ had cursed Western rock artists like Springsteen. And then all of a sudden they were welcoming him. It looked like they were caving in to the shifting values of young people. The FDJ was hoping a taste of Western artists like Springsteen might make the young people content."

East Germany frowned upon rock 'n' roll throughout the 1950s and 1960s because it was considered "decadent-negative" by the ruling SED party. Many of the post-war East German leaders who had spent World War II in exile in Moscow viewed rock music as self-indulgent and a symbol of the Western cosmopolitan lifestyle that they rejected. In their eyes rock music was a dangerous American cultural weapon designed to seduce and corrupt young East Germans and turn them away from Socialism. A telling illustration of that East German attitude towards rock 'n' roll can be seen in an earlier East German dictionary: "Rock 'n' roll. Originating in the U.S.A., it is an exaggerated form of boogie; it seduces young people to excesses; in West Germany it serves as an instrument for psychological warfare that distracts young people from political issues."

Ironically, while East German leaders were trying to keep rock out as long as they could, they made it all the more interesting—a "forbidden fruit" for young and even mildly rebellious East Germans. Young East Germans were starved for rock 'n' roll long before Springsteen came to town. In 1969, for instance, there was a frenzy over a bogus report that the Rolling Stones were coming to play for East Berlin. Rumor had it that the band was going to play a concert on top of a nineteen-story West Berlin high rise, the Springer publishing building, some 270 feet above the Berlin Wall, on October 7, 1969. The tower was built in 1965 by West Berlin's Axel Springer publishing house and stood directly next to the Wall, which the publisher loathed.

It's not hard to see where the rumor started. Springer had used the high-visibility of the top floor of his office tower for a scrolling news banner that beamed Western news headlines in giant letters across the heart of East Berlin, so that East Germans could read Western news bulletins unfiltered by Communist censors. But there would be no Rolling Stones concert on the Springer building that day. "It was only a rumor, but it was enough to get thousands of young people coming from all across East Germany and they gathered en masse near the Wall opposite the Springer building," says Jochen Staadt, a scholar of East German political history at the Free University of Berlin. "There were hundreds of people who were waiting for what they thought would be a concert." Some of the young people began chanting "Die Mauer muss weg" (the Wall must go) when the police intervened and started arresting those who wouldn't leave.

Rock music became a cherished outlet for many younger East Germans to express their hopes and dreams of a freer life, doubtlessly in part because the totalitarian government was so viscerally opposed to it. One of the most precious commodities an East German youth could possess in the 1970s and 1980s was an original Western rock album. Original records from Western performers such as ABBA, Tina Turner, the Beatles, Michael Jackson, the Rolling Stones, or Bruce Springsteen were a veritable currency in their own right in East Germany. Any East German fortunate enough to have relatives visiting from the West might hope for a pair of jeans or, better yet, an original album whenever Christmas or birthdays rolled around. And because East German senior citizens were allowed to travel to the West, many young East Germans hoped their grannies might bring back albums upon their return to East Germany, or Western currency for them to buy albums or other imported products in Intershops, special stores that catered to Westerners and only accepted Western currencies.

With the Communist Party gradually succumbing to the reality of the situation in East Germany and relaxing its opposition to rock, there were suddenly dozens of East German bands that formed in the 1970s and 1980s. These bands, though, were still subject to tight state controls. Their lyrics were scrutinized in advance and approved by the state before the bands could obtain the official permits required for public performances. Some East German bands, such as the Klaus Renft Combo that was popular in the 1970s, were later banned because of lyrics that went too far on taboo subjects—even though that is precisely what many East German audiences were so eager to hear. The Klaus Renft Combo got into trouble with the government in 1975, when it tried to perform a song called "Die Rockballade vom kleinen Otto" (The Rock Ballad of Little Otto), about a young man who died trying to escape to West Germany. The band was immediately banned, and several members were even sent to prison for the lyrics that were indirectly critical of the regime.

East German rulers had sanctioned unofficial public opinion polls that offered a telling snapshot of the mood in the country, and they knew they were losing the battle. Jochen Staadt has studied the unpublished polls and says they were fairly accurate, but only because they were conducted anonymously. "By the mid-1980s, they knew from those surveys that the young people were turning against them," says Staadt. "By the 1980s, more than seventy percent of the young people told the survey takers that they were listening only to West German radio and Western pop music and spurning East German media entirely."

East German young people rejecting the GDR's state-run radio stations were listening instead to readily available Western radio stations—like West Berlin networks RIAS (Radio in the American Sector), BFSB (the British Forces Broadcasting Service), SFB (Station of Free Berlin), and Bavaria's Bayern3. Listening to Western radio or watching West German TV was in itself an act of tacit rebellion for many East Germans, remembers Birgit Walter, then a thirty-six-year-old journalist who covered the concert for the East German newspaper *Berliner Zeitung*, where she still works today. She was among the vast majority of East Germans who never listened to East German radio or watched East German TV. "I couldn't stand the garbage they had on the air," she says. "It was all a pack of lies and total nonsense. You could hear the propaganda coming through the instant you switched the radio on. I absolutely refused to listen to any East German broadcasts."

From the Communist point of view, tuning into Western broadcasts was tantamount to fraternizing with the enemy. In the 1950s and 1960s, civic-minded East Germans even patrolled their neighborhoods and reported to the Stasi any East Germans who dared point their rooftop TV antennas toward the West. But by the 1980s, almost every rooftop antenna was pointed westward. In fact, that was one of the easiest ways for people in East Germany to get their directional bearings: just by looking up at which way the antennas were pointing, they could usually easily figure out which way was west. To help and to encourage East Germans tape albums of popular Western artists, many West German radio stations near the East German border even broadcast a special commercial-free "Mitschnittservice" (record-along sessions) during which their East German listeners could tape entire albums without any comments or interruptions from DJs between songs.

In 1987, tension was increasing between the younger generations and the elderly hardliners running East Germany. Younger East Germans wanted more freedom and the better life that they saw was becoming possible in other Eastern Bloc states. The strain erupted in some scattered street violence near the Berlin Wall in the summer of 1987—a rare outburst of violence in a tightly controlled country. The source of the trouble was music—open-air concerts in West Berlin, on the other side of the Wall.

Several top British acts, headlined by David Bowie, Genesis, and the Eurythmics, performed in a series of open-air concerts next to the Berlin Wall, on a field in front of the Reichstag in West Berlin, Germany's historic parliament building. The concerts were held in honor of Berlin's 750th anniversary, on three successive evenings from June 6 to June 8, 1987—within earshot of adjacent East Berlin neighborhoods. The concert series was organized by West Berlin promoter Peter Schwenkow and called "Concert for Berlin." The title itself was a provocative gesture to Communist East German sensibilities, suggesting a pan-Berlin audience instead of what would have been the more politically correct banner "Concert for West Berlin."

Although there was no official announcement in East Berlin about the concerts taking place on the field just west of the Wall, news spread throughout East Germany, thanks to concert-sponsor and -broadcaster RIAS, a popular radio network founded in 1946 by the U.S. occupational authorities in their southwest Berlin sector. RIAS became an important source of information and entertainment for millions of Germans both in the East and West during the Cold War, and was the most popular foreign radio network in East Germany. Many East Germans thought the "Concert for Berlin" might be their once-in-a-lifetime chance to hear a fragment of live music from David Bowie or Genesis from across the Wall, where the stage and loudspeakers were set up at the western edge of the Reichstag field, pointed east. Additional loudspeakers were set up at the eastern edge of the field, next to the Wall.

Schwenkow, now a prominent member of the conservative Christian Democratic Party, was thirty-four when he produced the concert in 1987. "I wanted to rile the people in power over there in East Berlin," Schwenkow admits, still proud of his anti-Communist stance. "I had my own little private war going on against them." A decade before the "Concert for Berlin," Schwenkow had been a young concert stagehand when he was suddenly detained at gunpoint by East German border guards for asking too many questions. The guards interrogated him for hours after he asked why two crew members of Tina Turner's road show had died in a mysterious car crash on an East German highway on their way to a concert in West Berlin just a few days earlier. Schwenkow later found out that their car had crashed into an East German car that had broken down on the highway and was standing in the road in the middle of the night, without any lights on. "I hated the East German authorities after that for holding me at gunpoint just for asking questions. Organizing a concert years later in front of the Reichstag was one way I was able to annoy them."

Schwenkow ended up losing 200,000 DM (West German marks, about $100,000) on the Berlin concert series. He says part of the reason for the loss was because tickets were relatively inexpensive, at 50 DM ($25), for all three days. He also blames it on the fact that West Berlin was an island of two million people without any surrounding region from which to draw a paying audience, because everyone who lived in the GDR was locked out of West Berlin by the Wall and people from Western Germany had to travel hundreds of miles to West Berlin. On top of his losses, Schwenkow later even had to pay a 45,000 DM fine to West Berlin authorities for violating noise ordinances—the sound level recorded at the concerts was three times over the maximum level permitted. But Schwenkow laughs about the fine now and says it was worth it. He's also proud of the fact that the artists who participated in the "Concert for Berlin" had agreed to allow their performances to be radio-broadcast by RIAS and beamed into East Germany.

About a quarter of the loudspeakers on the concert grounds were pointed away from the West Berlin crowd and toward the Berlin Wall and East Berlin, Schwenkow says. Each evening from June 6 to June 8, 1987, as 80,000 watched the concerts in West Berlin, there were also several thousand East Germans gathered just a few hundred yards away, on the east side of the Wall near the Brandenburg Gate. Some had traveled to East Berlin from far across East Germany, hoping to hear the music by performers they could not see from behind the twelve-foot Wall. Cindy Opitz was an American studying in East Germany. She and a group of friends had traveled from Rostock to listen to the concert from behind the Wall in East Berlin. They found a spot near an inner courtyard where they thought they would be able to hear the sound from West Berlin. But when they saw someone flashing their apartment lights on and off—presumably a signal to the police that a group of people were gathering in conspiratorial fashion near the Wall—they scattered and ran. One of her East German friends was on leave from the East German army and could have gotten into serious trouble if he had been caught with an American. Opitz and her East German fiancé, Torsten, made it to a nearby hotel, the Metropol. They checked in and listened to the Eurythmics from an open window.

The concert put East Germany's security forces on high alert, due to the potential for problems as masses of East Germans got close to the death strip set up on the east side of the Berlin Wall, and to the threat of violent incidents near the Wall. Memories of 1953 lingered, when a spontaneous and poorly organized rebellion led by East German workers against Communist rule was crushed in the same area. At least fifty-five people were killed when the uprising was violently put down with the help of Soviet tanks. Thousands of East Germans were sentenced to long prison terms. East Germany accused RIAS and the CIA of inciting the short-lived 1953 rebellion.

What might happen in 1987 if countless thousands of East Germans straining to listen to the concerts suddenly started making a move toward the Wall? Would there be violence and bloodshed while West Berlin, the Western media, West Berliners, and Western tourists watched from the other side? Might large numbers of East Germans gathered near the Wall try to overwhelm a smaller number of East German border guards? Things did turn ugly during the 1987 "Concert for Berlin," when East German police used force to clear the area of people whose only "crime" was listening to the music. They were beaten back for ignoring an order to leave the "sensitive" areas where some streets such as Unter den Linden and Schiffbauerdamm ran right up to the Wall.

The police used truncheons and electric stun guns against their compatriots. Matthias Beck, a twenty-one-year-old carpenter, had traveled from Leipzig to East Berlin to try to listen to the music from behind the Berlin Wall and remembers getting beaten by police. "I was able to hear little fragments of the music, depending on which way the wind was blowing at the moment," said Beck, who came back to East Berlin a year later to see Springsteen in Weissensee. "But it didn't end well. I got a first-hand taste of the power of the state, up close and personal, right in the face. But the few bruises they gave me were nothing compared to what our parents' generation had to live through."

In an act of desperation, some of the East German music fans began chanting slogans, such as "Gorbachev! Gorbachev!"—hoping to stop the police beatings by invoking the name of the Soviet leader. They also chanted "Weg mit der Mauer" (the Wall must go) and "Wir wollen Freiheit" (we want freedom). While shouting these things might seem like a relatively mild act of civil disobedience to 21st-century readers, back in 1987 it could have led to a jail term in one of East Germany's infamous prisons or destroyed a person's career or any chance of being allowed to study at a university. About 200 East Germans were arrested on the spot after the scuffles near the Wall. It was a dark hour for the East German regime. Violence used against music fans flew completely in the face of the *perestroika* and *glasnost* reforms. Because it happened in such a high-profile area near the Berlin Wall, and because most East Germans had easy access to West German television and radio broadcasts, it did not take long for word and images of the beatings to spread across East Germany.

West Germany's ARD public television network was popular across most of East Germany. On the next night, ARD's East Germany correspondent Peter Merseburger gave a chilling report on the violent skirmishes that occurred during David Bowie's performance. "Street-fighting broke out in East Berlin last night, the likes of which the city has not seen for a long time," Merseburger said. "The police went on the attack against East German youth, who were shouting for the Wall to be torn down. It all started harmlessly, with hundreds of East German youth gathering peacefully near the Wall to hear some of the concert over in West Berlin, a few hundred meters away. But the East German state dispatched a massive security presence, which began arresting some of the youths. The situation quickly escalated, and shouts of 'Pigs!' filled the air. That led to more police reinforcements rushing in and an even larger show of force by the state. Journalists covering the incident were also beaten."

The report was broadcast to all of West Germany on the evening news and across the Berlin Wall to most of East Germany as well. Merseburger also noted that the official East German state news agency, ADN, called the reports "a fantasy and horror story made up by Western correspondents." Film clips included in Merseburger's report showed that to be untrue, however. In the footage, uniformed East German police are seen clubbing people on the street near the Brandenburg Gate.

Staadt, political historian at West Berlin's Free University, says it was a nightmare for the East German regime that the violence was filmed by Western reporters. "It was aggravating that West German journalists were there to witness it and report on it," he says. "Because it was on TV, they couldn't hide it or pretend it didn't happen. It was a major blemish on their international image, and that was something the East German regime absolutely hated."

Even loyal young Communists in the FDJ realized that beating innocent people who were only trying to listen to music was a disheartening step backwards. The FDJ sensed even more acutely after the violence that changes were needed and that a government so out of touch with its people that it had to beat up those whose only crime was listening to music was going to have bigger problems before long. "We saw what had happened in 1987 on West German TV," says Rainer Börner, an East German music producer who was cultural secretary for the FDJ back then. "It just increased our frustration about not being allowed to do what we wanted to do. It was an overly nervous reaction of a one-party state that was in over its head. Some of us realized we had to start offering something more." Despite the financial losses he suffered, Peter Schwenkow says the concerts in West Berlin were a great success in other ways, "I was glad to see that the East German authorities were getting so worked up about it. It was a great feeling." Right away he started making plans for another "Concert for Berlin" series a year later, in June 1988. Pink Floyd was signed up for June 16, and Michael Jackson was signed up for June 19.

East German authorities were nervous about the 1988 return

of open-air concerts at the Reichstag in West Berlin and eager to do whatever was in their power to prevent another outbreak of violence in such a sensitive area. They tried diplomatic channels at the federal government level, to try to exert pressure on Schwenkow. They complained to West German authorities that loud music from concerts staged near the Wall could cause vibrations and "endanger" the lives of critical-care patients in East Berlin's nearby Charité Hospital. They got local West Berlin officials to promise that no loudspeakers would be pointed east, over the Wall. But that was a promise the officials couldn't keep. After an official check of the speakers by local West Berlin authorities, crew members turned many of them around to face the east, Schwenkow recalls.

West Berlin authorities under then-mayor Eberhard Diepgen, a conservative Christian Democrat, "didn't have the courage to stand up to the East German pressure," Schwenkow says, still miffed by what he calls a lack of backbone by the West Berlin administration. "So they put very tight restrictions on us and came out the evening before the concert to check the decibel level of the sound system. After the officials were gone, a Pink Floyd truck drove up and added six loudspeaker platforms pointed east. We later heard from people in East Berlin that the Pink Floyd concert managed to rattle windows for many miles away, far into East Berlin."

In an internal report on the concerts, the Stasi complained it had been double-crossed by Diepgen. The West Berlin mayor's promise that no loudspeakers would be pointed toward East Berlin had been broken, and some loudspeakers had been aimed over the Wall. The Stasi report also noted that organizers had set up two additional sound stages close to the Wall, which "were clearly aimed at East Germany." The report added, however, that "thanks to the favorable wind conditions"—blowing from east to west—the level of sound that reached East Berlin was not as loud as they had feared.

East Germany tried other methods in advance to defuse tension over the West Berlin concerts. Before the Jackson concert, Gerald Ponesky, a young and progressive manager of an East German band and member of the Communist Party, tried to make arrangements with the West German organizers for the Jackson performance in West Berlin to be projected on a giant screen set up in

East Berlin. This would enable Easterners to follow the concert at a location away from the Berlin Wall—but with a two-minute delay, in case censors needed to cut "provocations" out of the broadcast. Despite talks with West Berlin concert organizers, Ponesky's efforts ultimately proved unsuccessful. "The FDJ knew they had to do something to improve their image in East Germany, and they realized that there could be a lot of stress with Jackson's concert right behind the Wall in West Berlin," recalls Ponesky, who several weeks earlier came up with the idea of trying to get Springsteen to come to East Berlin and had been pushing hard for the idea to the various East German authorities. "That's why there was some interest for a while from high up in the Communist Party to look into the idea of an East Berlin video broadcast of Jackson's concert." Schwenkow, for his part, did mull over the idea of putting up a video wall in East Berlin, so that East Germans could see Jackson perform, but he eventually rejected it. "I didn't want to have anything to do with those people running East Germany," he says. "I didn't want to help them with anything."

East German officials eventually realized that the best way to divert the young people's attention away from the West Berlin concerts might be to stage its own series of summer rock concerts—at a venue a safe distance away from the Wall. The FDJ suggested holding summer rock concerts in the Weissensee district, on a former horse racing track that was turned into a cycling track with a giant vacant lot next to it. The location was about six miles to the northeast of the Brandenburg Gate, in the heart of East Berlin, and about three miles due east of the Berlin Wall. It was certainly a diversionary tactic to keep East Germans away from the Berlin Wall area. Still, the concerts were well received by young East Germans and succeeded in temporarily taking pressure away from East German security forces at the Berlin Wall.

On June 19, 1988, the same night Michael Jackson was playing in West Berlin, Canadian rock star Bryan Adams played hits like *Summer of '69* to a crowd of 120,000 East Germans at Weissensee. Several thousand Jackson fans from East Germany still gathered near the Wall to listen to Jackson's West Berlin concert, and the level of nervousness on the part of East German officials remained high. But the situation was nowhere near as tense as a year earlier, and there were no outbreaks of violence reported.

"Everything must be done to prevent any risks on East Germany's national border because any incidents there would be highly sensitive politically," the Stasi recorded after Jackson's June 19 concert, in a report dated June 28, 1988. "That is why it is imperative to always have sufficient numbers of security forces stationed there." The report also noted that the East Berlin concerts in Weissensee were not quite attractive enough to fully neutralize the West Berlin concerts in front of the Reichstag: "The international standing of Michael Jackson and the Pink Floyd group could not be completely negated by the offerings in Weissensee."

The Stasi counted about 3,000 East Germans gathered near the Wall to hear Pink Floyd on June 16, and a similar number for the Michael Jackson concert on June 19. As a precautionary measure, the Stasi had a total of 5,000 security forces on hand to prevent a repeat of the trouble that happened in 1987. "There were about 3,000 people, including about 500 who are known as negative-decadent elements," the report said of the situation in East Berlin while Pink Floyd was playing just a few blocks away in West Berlin. "Alongside those in front of the Brandenburg Gate who appeared to be genuinely interested in the music, there were also negative-decadent elements who, without doubt, represented the greatest threat. The situation was complicated because pressure from those genuinely interested and the negative-decadent elements sometimes overwhelmed the extra barriers set up by the security forces. That meant reinforcements from uniformed security forces had to be called in to secure the barriers. The use of supplemental aid devices, such as truncheons, was not necessary."

Above: Jon Landau, Springsteen's long-time manager, in a recent photo. Below: Gerald Ponesky, the driving force within the East German FDJ behind the concert. He watches the 2008 European soccer championship.

Chapter 4
The Tricky Part

The hungry and the hunted explode into rock 'n' roll bands. That face off against each other out in the street down in Jungleland
                                                                —Jungleland

It was during this period of heightened anxiety in East Germany over the West Berlin concerts at the Wall in June 1988 when Springsteen manager Jon Landau contacted West German promoter Marcel Avram to ask for his help in getting Springsteen a concert in East Berlin. Landau remembers it being surprisingly easy, all of a sudden, to put together the East Berlin show, even at such a late date. "It all got put together very fast," Landau said of the July 19 East Berlin concert date added to the schedule. The tour was already in full swing. Landau says Springsteen and his entourage were eager to play in East Berlin but had no plans to go behind the Iron Curtain with the aim of starting a revolution. "It wasn't like we all thought it was the greatest idea we ever had. It was more like 'Hey, that makes sense. Let's go do that.' It was a great show we were doing at the time, and everyone was happy to perform in East Berlin."

As with much of the history of the Cold War, there were usually two sides to the story—differing accounts in the East and West. Not surprisingly, the East German view about how Springsteen ended up in East Berlin in July 1988 is different from the Western view: According to the Eastern story, some young Communist leaders came up with the idea in June to invite Springsteen. They faxed him an invitation. And Springsteen came.

By fortunate coincidence, at the very same time that Landau was trying to find out whether East Berlin would allow Springsteen to play there, the FDJ wanted to sign him up to play at the summer rock festival in Weissensee and simply sent him an invitation. The FDJ was desperately trying to keep young East Germans committed to Communism, especially since internal opinion polling showed that disenchantment among young people was on the rise. Opening up East Germany to a bit of Western rock 'n' roll was seen as a positive step toward improving sentiment. The FDJ thought that landing a major Western rock star like Springsteen to perform in East Germany would help show the younger generations that things were changing and could get better. To their surprise and delight, he said "yes," and that's how they succeeded in booking one of the world's biggest rock stars.

"We wanted Springsteen because he was a major star around the world and not just another has-been," says Roland Claus, a former leader in the FDJ. It was a rather random and somewhat unsophisticated "this-is-a-long-shot" way to offer him a gig in East Berlin, but as good fortune would have it, Springsteen wanted East Berlin just as badly as East Berlin wanted Springsteen.

In Germany today, Gerald Ponesky is credited with having the idea to get Springsteen to East Berlin. Even in 1988, at the age of thirty-five, the hard-charging, fast-talking and quick-thinking Ponesky was a mover and shaker well ahead of his time. In 1988, he was working as the manager of a popular East German band called "Wir" (We). He was also a member in good standing of the Communist Party. His father, Hans-Georg Ponesky, was a well-known TV show host in East Germany. Like many younger East Germans, Ponesky saw an urgent need for reform.

An engaging man, Ponesky says he was the first to have the idea to invite Springsteen for a concert in East Berlin. It was in early June 1988, and East German Communist officials had summoned him to a last-minute assignment in Poland to rig up sound equipment for a speech that East German ruler Erich Honecker was planning to deliver in the city of Wroclaw, which until 1945 was part of Germany and is still called Breslau in Germany. On the night before the speech, Honecker's staff discovered, to their dismay, that the local Polish sound equipment was of extraordinarily poor quality, and they were afraid it would make their boss sound terribly inaudible. Ponesky got an urgent call in East Berlin, asking if he could somehow round up enough loudspeakers and sound equipment to help make Honecker sound more like an important leader than a rasping old man during his speech the next day. As a well-connected rock band manager, Ponesky got the job done.

"The sound equipment in Poland was horrible. It was a big venue, and everyone knew that Honecker's voice tended to get hoarse and squeaky after about two sentences in a big place like that—so they needed quick help getting better equipment," says Ponesky. "In East Germany, everyone knew that rock bands usually had the best sound equipment. Most of it actually came to us second-hand from the West. So the FDJ called and asked if I could help out. I called around to bands all across East Germany and got the equipment together, loaded it on a truck, and drove through the night to Breslau. We got it all set up in time for Honecker's speech. The event was a success, and everyone was happy."

Ponesky and his friends were in a celebratory mood after the speech that evening, wandering around Breslau, when he saw a giant poster of Springsteen hanging on a wall in a shop. "I thought 'Wow, that's it! That's the guy we need to get to play a concert in East Germany! We've got to try to get him to play for us.' So we just started talking about it that night over a few beers, and that's how the idea took off," Ponesky recalls. He believed in East Germany and hoped for reforms that would make the Communist country a more livable place. He was optimistic that Springsteen's reputation as an artist interested in the little people of the world would be helpful in getting the necessary approvals from Communist leaders higher up.

Today, Ponesky is the head of a thriving event management company in Berlin, and that is the version of the story that he tells fondly and that has been repeated in German newspaper accounts over the years. There is some truth to it, but it is only half the story—the East German version. As a rock band manager, Ponesky knew the written and unwritten rules about performing in East Germany and knew that bands could be quickly disbanded, outlawed, and even jailed by the state if their lyrics broke any of those rules. He also knew it would be difficult to persuade the "powers that be" in East Germany to let in an American rock 'n' roll star. But he thought

Springsteen had the right sort of working-class image of someone who might be palatable to the geriatric hardliners in control of the country. And the resourceful Ponesky had a plan to get Springsteen past the die-hards who might try to veto the appearance of the American rock star. He also suspected that there were red lines that his West German counterparts wouldn't cross. His scheme certainly helped the concert win approval, but it all nearly blew up on him and everyone who wanted to see Springsteen in East Berlin.

"There was this rumor going around that Springsteen had once donated a printing press to Nicaragua," Ponesky recalls. He admits he doesn't know where the rumor started or whether it was even true. But it sounded reasonable enough at the time, and as far as he knew Springsteen had never denied it—although maybe only because he'd never heard it. "That sounded like a good basis to start with. And it seemed quite plausible. We knew the FDJ wanted to come up with something special for the young people in East Germany, who were growing impatient. We knew if we were going to try to get someone that it had to be someone who was really big right then, not someone who was already past their prime. We'd already had more than a few of those over-the-hill acts from the West. So we approached the FDJ, telling them we could make a connection between a Springsteen concert and East German solidarity with Nicaragua." At this time—two years after the Iran-Contra-affair had come to light—solidarity with Nicaragua and the governing Sandinistas had grown into a rallying cry not only in the Eastern bloc but also among leftists in Western Europe.

Ponesky felt that the plan to tie Springsteen to Nicaragua was his best shot. "Ein Herz für Nikaragua" (Have a heart for Nicaragua) would be the concert's slogan that would surely help whisk it through the approvals process in the East German government. But Ponesky quite rightly sensed he couldn't tell his West German counterparts the details about it just yet. "The West German concert organizers understood that we would have to do certain things to get the Communist regime to accept it, otherwise they knew there would be no chance of it being approved," Ponesky says. "We knew about those old rumors about the printing press in Nicaragua, so that's how we came up with a slogan." Ponesky recalls that his West German counterparts at first didn't seem especially eager to know about the nitty-gritty details of his plans to get approval. "I knew we'd have no chance if we went ahead and told the FDJ it was the 'Tunnel of Love Tour.' It was the only chance we had. All I could do was hope it would somehow work out."

Ponesky now acknowledges it was a risk-filled strategy, but the FDJ was determined to brighten the lives of young East Germans and he wanted to give the FDJ the necessary arguments to persuade the hard-line Communist East German government to allow the Springsteen concert to take place. "We had the hope that once Springsteen found out about that he would perhaps just accept it," Ponesky says. And if he didn't, they believed they would be able to figure out a way to make it possible to go ahead with the concert without upsetting Springsteen and yet still satisfy the powers that be in the East German Communist Party.

In those pre-internet days, decades before the spread of social media, it was not possible for most ordinary East Germans to simply pick up a telephone and call across the Iron Curtain to West Germany. In 1988, relatively few people in East Germany even had a home telephone, a deliberate tactic on the part of the totalitarian state to prevent dissent from gathering momentum. But Ponesky, a Communist Party member with an important job to do, was given access to a special telephone line in an East German government building that was cleared to place telephone calls to the West. He was put through to West Germany, to speak with the concert organizers there. "I asked if there would be a possibility of getting Springsteen to play in East Berlin. They called me back and said they were interested, so we got started negotiating right away."

Negotiations between concert organizers in East and West Berlin quickly moved forward but were in some ways awkward. These were two completely different worlds. The key questions, such as the compensation issue and who would build the stage and the lighting equipment, were resolved relatively easily. Unlike other Western acts that insisted on fees in a convertible currency, Springsteen was willing to play in essence for free. That was a huge relief for East Germany, Ponesky says. "We didn't have any Western money available for the concerts, and most of the Western

The Stasi security police kept close tabs on Springsteen. This preconcert analysis on the opposite page says that Springsteen's live shows were a "special experience" for the audience thanks to his solid musical skills and his powerful songs about the "darker aspects of reality in America." He has become a "living rock legend" inside and outside the United States with his 1984 album "Born in the USA" that sold 17 million records. And "5 million fans saw him in sold out stadiums in two world tours, one in 1985, and a second one starting in Febrary 1988."

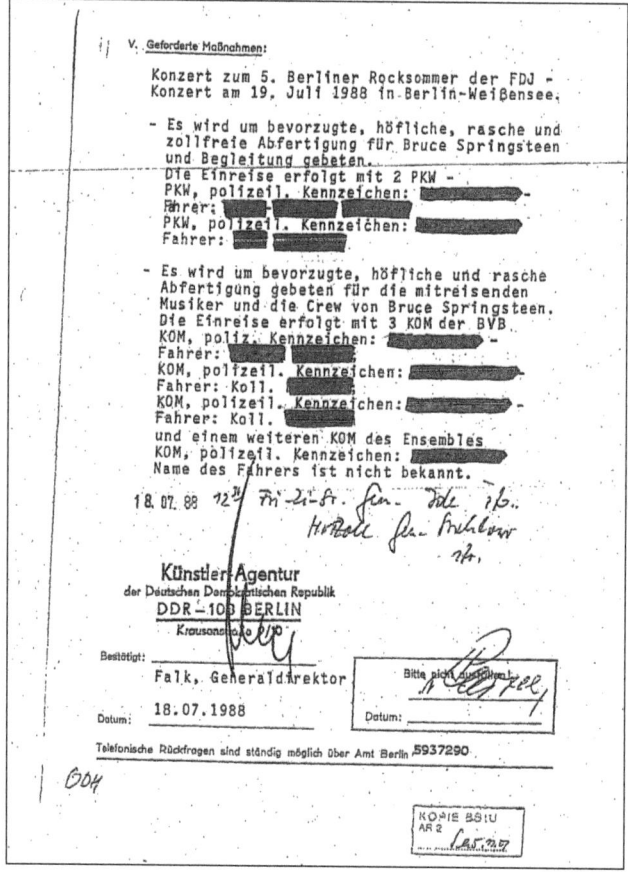

In this note above, the East German Artists Agency urged the notoriously nasty guards at the border at Checkpoint Charlie crossing to be polite and speedy when processing the entry of Springsteen and his band.

```
Kurzcharakteristik von Bruce Springsteen                            4
- geboren am 23. 02. 1949 im Staat New Jersey, USA
- gilt heute als die unangefochtene Spitze zeitgenössischer
  Rockmusik in der Welt
- seine Texte - von harten, ungeschönten Songs über die
  Schattenseiten der amerikanischen Wirklichkeit bis hin
  zu poetischen Balladen - haben ebenso zu seinem Erfolg
  beigetragen, wie solides musikalisches Handwerk, das
  besonders seine Liveshows zu einem besonderen Erlebnis
  werden lassen
- vor allem durch seine Live-Konzerte wurde er dreimal zum
  Lieblingsstar des amerikanischen Publikums gewählt
- entwickelt sich auch außerhalb der USA immer mehr zu
  einer lebenden Rocklegende; seine Rock-LP "Born in the
  U. S. A." (1984) könnte sich in den USA sieben Wochen
  als Nr. 1 halten und gilt mit weltweit 17 Millionen ver-
  kaufter Exemplare als eine der erfolgreichsten aller
  Zeiten
- insgesamt 5 Millionen Fans sahen ihn in immer ausver-
  kauften Stadien und Hallen bei seiner 1. Welttournee
  1985; seine 2. Welttournee läuft seit Februar 1988
```

This Stasi document at right informing the guards at the border crossing at Checkpoint Charlie—as it was known in West Berlin, or Zimmerstrasse, as it was known in East Berlin—that the "international rock star" Bruce Springsteen would be arriving by car between 3:15 p.m. and 4:00 p.m. on July 18.

BStU
000345

Maßnahmen zur inhaltlichen Ausgestaltung des Solidaritätskonzerts am 19. 7. 1988 mit Bruce Springsteen und der "E Street Band" (USA)

Das Konzert mit Bruce Springsteen, das am 9. Jahrestag der Sandinistischen Revolution stattfindet, ist der Solidarität mit Nikaragua gewidmet. Zugleich ist bei der inhaltlichen Vorbereitung zu berücksichtigen, daß das Botha-Regime den 19. 7. als Hinrichtungstermin für die Sharpeville-Sechs festgelegt hat.

Maßnahmen zur inhaltlichen Darstellung der Solidarität mit Nikaragua

1. Am 7. 7. 1988 erscheint in der "Jungen Welt" eine Seite, auf der Informationen über den 5. Berliner Rocksommer der FDJ und den damit verbundenen Solidaritätsgedanken gegeben werden.
Vorschlag für den Titel: "5. Berliner Rocksommer der FDJ: Nikaragua im Herzen". Eventuelle inhaltliche Elemente: Veranstaltungsübersicht des gesamten Rocksommers; Solidarität mit Nikaragua (Solidaritätserlös nach Abschluß des gesamten Rocksommers zugunsten des FDJ-Krankenhauses "Karl Marx" in Managua; Eröffnungsveranstaltung am 9. Jahrestag der Sandinistischen Revolution usw.); Beitrag über Bruce Springsteen sowie weitere Mitwirkende am 5. Berliner Rocksommer der FDJ. Ferner erscheint in diesem Kontext eine Ankündigung des Kartenverkaufs für das Bruce-Springsteen-Konzert (s. Anlage 1). Analog sollte in der "Berliner Zeitung", in der BZA sowie DT 64 verfahren werden.

verantw.: Redaktion Junge Welt
Bezirksleitung Berlin
Abteilung Kultur
Abteilung Agitation

2. Die Bühne ist mit folgenden Elementen versehen:

Überbühnenhänger: "Bruce Springsteen"
Seitenhänger: - "5. Berliner Rocksommer der FDJ"
- "Solidarität mit Nikaragua"

Für die Gestaltung des Bühnenbereichs werden die Farben der Sandinistischen Revolution Rot und Schwarz verwendet. Zugleich werden Fahnen der FDJ und der Hauptstadt Berlin gesetzt.

verantw.: Gestalterkollektiv

This Stasi report says that the slogan of Springsteen's concert, which marked the ninth anniversary of the Sandinistas' victory, was solidarity with Nicaragua. It explains the contents of the banners—the same red and black that the Sandinistas used—and where they were to be placed on the stage. The Stasi also dictates that the announcement of the concert should in the Junge Welt *newspaper, including the headline "5th Berlin rock summer—Nicaragua in our hearts." It should also be released in other party media;* Berliner Zeitung, *the BZ, and DT 64 radio. Proceeds from the concert would be donated to the Karl Marx Hospital in Managua.*

```
Zentraler Operativstab                                    LE 30/311 Bl.v. 20.7
                                    BSTU                  AKG/6040/1 s
                                    0024                  Berlin, 20. 7. 1988

Ergebnisse der politisch-operativen Sicherung des Eröffnungskonzertes des 5. Berliner Rock-
sommers der FDJ mit dem nordamerikanischen Sänger Bruce Sprinsteen auf den Sportplätzen an
der Radrennbahn in Berlin-Weißensee am 19. 7. 1988

Im Ergebnis der festgelegten politisch-operativen Maßnahmen zur Sicherung des Eröffnungskon-
zertes des 5. Berliner Rocksommers der FDJ mit einem Konzert des nordamerikanischen Sängers
Bruce Springsteen auf den Sportplätzen an der Radrennbahn in Berlin-Weißensee wurden durch
die zuständigen Diensteinheiten der BV Berlin und der KD Berlin-Weißensee im engen Zusammen-
wirken mit der DVP, dem Veranstalter und den gesellschaftlichen Kräften in den Sicherungsbe-
reichen und deren Umfeld eine hohe öffentliche Ordnung und Sicherheit gewährleistet.

Vor, während und nach dem Konzert gab es keine Vorkommnisse bzw. Zuführungen. Die Besucher
des Konzertes verhielten sich diszipliniert.

Die Verkehrsorganisation zum An- und Abtransport der Besucher entsprach den Anforderungen.

Das Veranstaltungsgelände wurde um 15.12 Uhr für die Besucher geöffnet. Um 19.03 Uhr begann
das Konzert und es endete um 23.00 Uhr. Es waren ca. 160 000 Besucher anwesend. Insgesamt
wurde 1 763 mal medizinisch Hilfe geleistet, davon mußten 19 Personen stationär behandelt
werden. Von den 19 Personen konnten 8 wieder entlassen werden.

Durch den Veranstalter wurden 74 ausländische Korrespondenten und Techniker akkreditiert.
Darunter 5 Fernsehstationen aus der BRD und Berlin (West): ARD, ZDF, SAT 1, Eurica und SFB/TV.

Das Mitglied des Politbüros des ZK der SED, Genosse Egon KRENZ, weilte in der Zeit von 20.10
Uhr bis 20.33 Uhr auf dem Veranstaltungsgelände. Während dieser Zeit war die Sicherheit des
Genossen KRENZ ständig gewährleistet.

Weitere Gäste des Konzertes waren Vertreter der Botschaften aus Nikaragua und der USA.

Verteiler: Genosse Generaloberst Mittig
           Genosse Generalleutnant Neiber
           Genosse Generalleutnant Schwanitz
           HA II, VII, IX, XX, PS
           ZAIG, BV Berlin, ZOS
```

This report to Stasi generals describes the security at the concert of the "North American singer Bruce Springsteen" at the cycling track in Weissensee. It praises the way that the various East German organizations that were involved in securing the venue. "There were no incidents before, during and after the concert and there were no arrests. The people attending the concert were highly disciplined." The concert began at 7:03 p.m. sharp and ended at 11 p.m. There were 160,000 spectators; 1,763 needed medical treatment of some kind, of which 19 were taken to a hospital—all but eight were soon released. The Stasi noted there were 74 foreign correspondents at the concert. Egon Krenz, the leader of the East German youth organization FDJ, arrived at 8:10 p.m. and stayed until 8:33 p.m. "During that time comrade Krenz had the highest level of security protecting him at all times." Guests of the concert included representatives of the embassies from both Nicaragua and the USA.

artists didn't want to play for East German money." The organizational issues, however, turned out to be minor in comparison to what was involved in persuading the Communist authorities in East Germany to let Springsteen in to play.

Landau says Springsteen did the concert for free, and East Germany picked up the cost of the concert, building the stage, and providing the sound system. "I don't recall us being paid," he said. "If we got some money at all, it was only to help defray the costs of doing the show. I really don't think we got paid anything. It was not a regular show for us." Roland Claus, the FDJ leader who helped organize the concert, confirms Springsteen's compensation was minimal. "We paid very little, almost nothing," he says. Many of the Western artists accepted a grand piano made in East Germany or Meissen porcelain as compensation, but Claus says Springsteen did not ask for any of that. "The negotiations for the Springsteen concert were totally uncomplicated. There was no long contract, the things you see these days with twenty-five different clauses. The attitude was 'Let's just do it.' The East Germany side had the responsibility of getting the stage and sound system in place. We had to take care of all the technical details."

The FDJ was hugely proud of its coup. Arranging concerts with Western acts was a task that was usually the responsibility of the Künstler-Agentur der DDR (East German Artist Agency), a state monopoly that negotiated contracts for international artists and made sure foreign artists coming to East Berlin were treated well and got to their performances on time and without hassles. But it was the FDJ, eager to spruce up its deteriorating image among the East German youth, that was organizing the summer rock festivals in Weissensee and took the lead on Springsteen. "We thought we'd just send a fax out into the big wide world, say we were interested, and see what happens," said Claus, smiling at the memory of how naïve they had been in the FDJ. "We knew it was only a stab in the dark. It was sort of like sending off a fax to the moon to see what would happen. But it worked! We were all surprised to get a positive answer back right away." The FDJ had a bit of good fortune on its side in getting elderly men who disliked rock music to approve the concert, he says with a laugh:

"We were lucky that the old men at the top of the SED didn't seem to know much about Springsteen."

It was a challenge to get the approval needed from the Communist Party (SED)—which ruled everything in East Germany and was already uneasy about the changes and growing freedoms in other Eastern Bloc countries—but Claus managed to convince the East German rulers that it was a good idea to let Springsteen in to play. "We had general approval for the concert series but still had to get a separate permit for every single act," Claus recalls of tight grip the SED kept on the Weissensee concerts. "It obviously wasn't easy, and we had to fight hard to get permission, but we eventually succeeded. The higher-ups understood that rock music was international and if East Germany wanted to do something to improve the lot of young people, we'd have to try something."

The Stasi also kept close tabs on the planning for the concert. Stasi records note that the first meetings in East Berlin to discuss the Springsteen concert took place on June 29, 1988. The report advised against announcing the date of the concert right away, fearing it could cause disruption for an extended period in East Germany, and suggested first offering advance ticket sales at one central location in East Berlin—at the Werner-Seelenbinder Halle in Prenzlauer Berg, a sports complex that no longer exists.

Stasi records also show that the East German Communist Party's Central Committee set ticket prices at 20 East Marks, with expected production costs of about one million East Marks (about $500,000 at the official exchange rate). After expenses were met, all remaining proceeds were to be donated to the Nicaragua solidarity fund—and the "Carlos Marx Hospital" in Managua, named after Communist philosopher Karl Marx. The hospital was opened in 1985 as a solidarity project with East Germany. After German unification in 1990, the name of the German Jewish author of the "Communist Manifesto" was quietly dropped, and the hospital was renamed the "Hospital Aleman-Nicaraguense" (German-Nicaraguan Hospital).

East Germany did not officially announce the Springsteen concert until just one week before the July 19 concert date. The announcement on ADN, the official East German news agency, read: "The FDJ's fifth summer rock concert series will take place from

July 19 to 24, 1988. It will be an act of anti-imperialist solidarity with Nicaragua. The opening show on July 19 will be Bruce Springsteen and the E Street Band (USA) with a four-hour concert at the cycling track in Berlin-Weissensee." The Nicaragua connection, however, that made the concert acceptable to the ruling Communists in the first place would turn out to be a major obstacle that nearly jeopardized the whole show.

Conny Rudat—now married Günther—spent two days working as Springsteen's translator in East Berlin in 1988. In a recent photograph she holds the autographed album and "Tunnel of Love Tour Express-Tour" sweatshirt she got from Bruce.

Chapter 5
Journey to the Other Side

Man I ain't getting nowhere, I'm just living in a dump like this
—Dancing in the Dark

Getting the powers that ruled East Germany to agree to allow an American rock star like Springsteen to perform there was never going to be easy—not even in 1988, when there had been an appreciable thaw in the East German government's position on rock concerts. Yet the East German government was also eager to avoid a repeat of the embarrassing violence at the Berlin Wall that erupted a year earlier in 1987, when East German security used force to beat back hundreds of music fans trying to get closer to the Wall to listen to West Berlin rock concerts. Some of the more progressive elements in the regime were in favor of the idea of allowing in Western bands that the young people of East Germany were so eager to see and hear for themselves. Western bands, for their part, were eager to reach out to new fans on the other side of the Iron Curtain.

"The idea was that we'll let some Western musicians in to East Berlin to relieve some of the pressure that was building," said concert promoter Gerald Ponesky. So East Germany started letting in more Western acts—although East Germany's dearth of convertible currency meant talks to get some of the most popular bands did not get far. The Rolling Stones, for example, waited to play in the East until six weeks after the July 1990 *Währungsunion* (currency union)—when East Germans were allowed to trade in their East Marks for West Marks (DM)—so the band received concert proceeds in Western currency. Each of the 18,000 ticket-holders paid 43 DM (about $21) for the Rolling Stones concert at Weissensee on August 13, 1990, where Springsteen had played two years earlier for a crowd more than ten or even twenty times larger.

Not all Western performers waited, however. Bob Dylan was a harbinger of change in East Germany when he appeared in East Berlin on September 17, 1987, at a concert in Treptower Park. Dylan, who was forty-six in 1987, was popular in East Germany, thanks to his songs about protest against the Vietnam War, such as "Blowin' in the Wind" and "The Times They Are a-Changin'." But those who saw his lackluster performance that evening in East Berlin described the show as a massive disappointment. Dylan was anything but inspirational. He did not endear himself, either, by leaving quickly with nary a wave goodbye after playing just 14 songs in a little over an hour. He gave no encore and left the venue while the East Germans were still applauding for more.

In the next few months, more Western acts appeared in East Berlin. On March 7, 1988, British band Depeche Mode played in a small indoor arena in East Berlin for a concert to celebrate the FDJ's thirtieth anniversary. On June 1, 1988, Joe Cocker played an open-air concert to an audience of 80,000 at the Weissensee venue. And as mentioned earlier, on June 19, 1988, the same evening that Michael Jackson was singing in front of the Reichstag in West Berlin, Bryan Adams held his open-air concert at Weissensee, attended by about 120,000. The concerts in East Berlin were popular with the East German youth—and made it appear as if, at long last, things were changing for the better in their country. But that was all nothing compared to what would happen a month later in July.

Springsteen arrived in West Berlin on July 18, 1988, the day before the concert, with an entourage of twenty-five people that included his manager, band members, and the traveling crew. He had flown to West Berlin's main airport, Tegel—an inner-city airstrip quickly built at the start of the Cold War in 1948. While Tempelhof is the city's famous airport known for the Allied airlift that supplied West Berlin with food, fuel, and coal during the Soviet blockade of all routes from West Germany to Berlin, some American, British, and French planes also landed in Tegel to help keep West Berlin supplied and out of Communist hands.

Journey to the Other Side

Springsteen was driven across West Berlin to the main East–West border crossing at Friedrichstrasse, more commonly known as Checkpoint Charlie, to his hotel in East Berlin, just a few blocks north of the famous crossing. East and West Berlin were once parts of the same city, but after decades of division it felt like a different planet in the East, and anyone passing from the colorful streets of West Berlin to the drab and relatively lifeless avenues of Communist East Berlin could instantly feel the chill of the Cold War. Before Springsteen arrived, the East German Artist Agency had sent an advance notice to the Friedrichstrasse border guards, asking the normally gruff and impersonal security inspectors to be polite and friendly.

Springsteen and his crew checked into the Grand Hotel Berlin, a majestic building at the corner of Unter den Linden and Friedrichstrasse. The Grand Hotel Berlin was a palace of luxury in the heart of East Berlin, with 359 rooms and plush suites reserved for well-heeled visitors who paid in convertible currencies—in other words, Westerners. The standard nightly rate at the time was 270 DM, officially about $135, or the equivalent of an average East German's monthly wage at the GDR's official export rate of exchange—although East German currency was not accepted there.

East Germany used its handful of luxury, first-class hotels to obtain convertible currencies, such as West German marks, U.S. dollars, British pounds, French francs, and Japanese yen, from visiting foreigners. The Grand Hotel Berlin was one of them. It was built in 1987 on the corner of Friedrichstrasse and Unter den Linden. Before World War II, the Café Kranzler stood there, opposite the Café Bauer, both popular hangouts for artists and tourists. Next to the Kranzler was the "Kaisergalerie," a three-story, glass-ceilinged indoor mall with a concert hall, theater, and wax museum. The whole block was bombed to rubble in 1944. The ruins stood empty until 1957, when the GDR finally cleared the lot. Nearly three decades later, the lot became the site of the new hotel. The pride of East Germany was ceremoniously opened in 1987 by none other than East German ruler Erich Honecker himself. Now called the Grand Westin Hotel Berlin, it still has one of the most inviting hotel lobbies anywhere in Germany—a brightly lit, spacious area filled with chandeliers and a grand staircase leading up to the balcony and hotel rooms above.

Springsteen was in good spirits when he arrived in East Berlin on that afternoon in July 1988. He was looking forward to finally getting the chance he had dreamed of since his first visit in 1981. But his good mood quickly soured. Shortly after arriving in East Berlin, he and his management team learned—by chance—about the Communists' pro-Nicaragua branding of the concert.

Landau remembers relaxing with Springsteen in the plush lobby of the Grand Hotel Berlin when they finally found out about the Nicaragua ploy. "We arrived the day before the show and met the various East German people who were putting the show together and working on everything. I remember Bruce and I were sitting on a couch in the lobby, just chatting, and this very nice young man came over and said, 'On behalf of the Communist Youth Organization, we want to thank Bruce for doing this concert to oppose the U.S. war in Nicaragua,'" Landau says. "Well, the problem with that was that it was completely new to us. That wasn't the purpose for doing the show," Landau says.

It was a disturbing discovery, just one day before the concert. Springsteen was unhappy, worried that the concert he had so looked forward to might be put into jeopardy. Landau, whose job it was to handle issues like this, immediately tried to find out what was going on. "I went and found the senior person who was somewhere else in the hotel and asked him if I could see a ticket, the actual concert ticket, and there it was." The ticket read "Konzert für Nikaragua" (Concert for Nicaragua). Landau was startled and told the East German official that was not going to work. He told him that Springsteen doesn't allow his music to be used to endorse anything. Period. "As soon as I saw the tickets with the Nicaragua situation right on the face of the ticket, I said anything referencing that situation—posters, t-shirts—everything had to be removed from the concert site," says Landau. The worried East German official tried to calm Landau down, pointing out that it was completely natural in East Germany for concerts or big events to have some kind of message of solidarity or world peace attached. He told Landau it was merely a standard type of message of solidarity always attached to concerts in East Germany and that few East Germans even really took notice of such banners. "The East German official said, 'Oh, don't worry, this is no big deal in East Germany; this is like doing 'a concert for Pepsi' in the United States,'" says Landau, who even twenty-five years later still has trouble seeing any humor in the East German Communist official's comment. "I said, 'Well, look, first of all we don't do that either,' and I told him this is not right." Landau kept the pressure on the East Germans to fix the problem, fast.

For a few nervous moments it looked like the concert might even be canceled. Using Springsteen as a propaganda tool was simply anathema to everything he stood for and believed in. It was a major miscalculation by Communist East German officials, who might not have realized that just a few years earlier Springsteen had turned down a $12 million offer to let his song *Born in the USA* be used in an ad campaign for Chrysler. There was no chance that he was going to let himself be used as a tool for East German propaganda. As much as Springsteen wanted to play in East Berlin, he would never allow himself to be part of an endorsement for Nicaragua. Landau says he would not really have gone so far as cancel the concert. But he adds: "I didn't mind if our East German colleagues thought that I might in order to make sure they were fully motivated to undo the Nicaragua situation as much as possible." Besides that, Landau observes with the hindsight of a quarter century, they both knew that Springsteen would have the final word on stage—with microphone in his hand—to clear up any misunderstandings about why he was in East Berlin.

But the tension soon dissipated thanks to the quick removal of most of the Nicaragua branding. Landau says the worried East Germans responded as he hoped they would. "We had to solve this problem in an acceptable fashion to us, which we did. The chief of the East German youth organization was a very professional man, and when he realized that there was a problem, he was very practical about it. He sent his top person with our top person to the field on the night before the show, to help remove all of those materials. We had all the signage pertaining to Nicaragua and so forth removed. The East German officials, once things were explained to them, were very accommodating."

At that late hour, though, there was nothing that could be done to change the printed tickets, which carried the "Concert for Nicaragua" label and had already been sold and distributed to some 160,000 people. The mood behind the scenes appeared to be so grim to some that even Kerwinski, the West German driver, thought for a while the show would be scrapped. "The first reaction from the management was 'We're leaving,'" Kerwinski says. "Landau wanted to leave right away, to pack up and get out of there. But Springsteen was more for staying and against leaving."

Conny Rudat is one of the East Berliners who remembers those tense moments about the pro-Nicaragua spin. The then twenty-eight-year-old single mother was assigned to work with Springsteen as an interpreter and liaison for the East German Artist Agency, the Künstler Agentur. Today, she writes for *The Economist* in Berlin and is married as Conny Günther. East Germany was always trying to enlist the support of Western artists for their various causes, whenever possible, Günther says, and this seemed like just another one of their standard attempts to put their Socialist stamp on the show. "You could see that Springsteen really wanted to go ahead and do the concert," she recalls. "He didn't want to get too involved in the management quarrel over it. He was staying calm through the whole thing. He was relaxed and it seemed that he was just eager to do the concert and be here."

That was certainly what Gerald Ponesky, the East German organizer, was hoping would happen. Ponesky was busy with preparations at the venue in Weissensee when he got word that Springsteen's tour manager was on the way out to have a look for himself—and that Springsteen's management was extremely perturbed after learning about the Nicaragua theme. Ponesky knew the moment of truth had come and that he had to think quickly.

"We were in a state of panic," Ponesky admits. "We were afraid the tour manager would come out and see all the banners and then turn right around and drive back to the hotel to call it all off. We were afraid that the concert could be cancelled." By that point, just a little more than a day before the concert, the buzz about Springsteen was already building across the country. Tens of thousands of people from East Germany's four corners—from along the shore of the Baltic Sea in the north, and from borders with Poland in the east, Czechoslovakia in the south, and West Germany in the west—were beginning to make the trek to Berlin and would create giant traffic jams the next day.

Ponesky knew it would take only about twenty minutes for the Springsteen tour manager to travel from the Grand Hotel Berlin in the center of East Berlin to the concert venue in Weissensee, a six-mile drive. Thinking quickly, he ordered his helpers to remove the giant "Nikaragua im Herzen" (Have a Heart for Nicaragua) banners that were hanging above and along the sides of the stage. Springsteen's road manager and the FDJ official then arrived to help take down whatever signs and posters that remained.

"The most important thing was getting the banners down from the stage," Ponesky says. He was ready for the confrontation over Nicaragua that he feared might happen sooner or later. But the Sandinista posters hanging up around the giant venue were all removed and the concert seemed to be saved. He admits he had been naïve. "But without the 'Nikaragua im Herzen' story, we knew we'd never get permission," Ponesky recalls. "We knew it breached the agreement. But we had to try something."

Reinhard Heinemann was head of the entertainment department at the East German Artist Agency at the time. He ended up intervening on behalf of Springsteen to the East German Communist authorities and told them that the labeling had not been part of the advance agreement and as a result should to be taken down. Heinemann said the authorities agreed with him and that it turned out that removing the banners was not a problem. "Everyone knew that there were certain little tricks like that you always had to do to get a concert approved in East Germany—either calling it a 'concert for world peace' or a 'concert for Nicaragua' or whatever," says Heinemann, who was thirty-nine then and now runs a shop for stamp collectors in Berlin's Prenzlauer Berg district. "It was no big deal to us. But it should have been clarified in advance and it wasn't."

Even though Springsteen and Landau didn't learn about the East German attempt to label the concert as an act of solidarity for Nicaragua until the day before the show, a Stasi report dated five days before the concert demonstrates that East Germany was clearly counting on Springsteen performing on behalf of Nicaragua. They were most likely only trying to fool themselves. The report in the Stasi files claims that an FDJ leader from the Culture Department met with Springsteen's manager in Frankfurt, West Germany, on July 12. "Based on the comrade's comments, East Germany's youth will be in for an invaluable artistic and musical experience that Springsteen and his accompanying band are very much looking forward to," the Stasi stated in a report for Central Department XX/2, dated July 14, 1988. "The artists have been informed about the political aspect of the concert (anti-imperialistic solidarity with Nicaragua) and have accepted it."

Like many Stasi documents, the report is most certainly a piece of fiction. Although the East Germans managed to quickly remove most of the concert propaganda in East Berlin, it was too late to change the tickets, so the incident still lingered in the air right up to the concert and fueled Springsteen's desire to set the record straight.

A close-up view of the official Tunnel of Love *sweatshirt.*

Chapter 6
STRANGE DAYS

Lives on the line where dreams are found and lost
I'll be there on time and I'll pay the cost
For wanting things that can only be found
In the darkness on the edge of town
   —Darkness on the Edge of Town

After Springsteen and Landau had dealt with the Nicaragua incident, "the Boss" and his band were eager to take advantage of their two days in East Berlin roam around the city more or less on their own, although their East German government minders were never very far away. "We had the chance to walk around and meet people," Landau recalls with fondness about the experience of being in East Berlin at such a pivotal moment not long before the Berlin Wall collapsed. "There was a great deal of change going on. You could see that everywhere. It was certainly exciting for us to be there at that time. It was an eye-opening experience to have those couple of days in East Berlin."

As always, Springsteen was eager to learn more about life in East Berlin. He spent several hours riding around with his girlfriend, Patti Scialfa, and Conny Günther from the East German Artist Agency. Günther recalls that she did most of the talking during her time with Springsteen because he kept bombarding her with all kinds of questions about the country and her life. "He was really interested in knowing what life was all about in East Berlin and how I was able to live behind the Iron Curtain," Günther says. "He was open-minded about East Germany and wasn't excessively negative about it. He told me that what he read in his newspapers about East Germany was that life is 'miserable' and life is 'gray.'

the middle of Berlin. In 1988, Unter den Linden led up to the Brandenburg Gate and the Berlin Wall—which was sealed off from the public by border guards, and was also where East German police had violently dispersed people gathering to hear concerts on the other side of the Wall during the summer of 1987. While he walked around, Springsteen ended up getting into conversations with several people. At one point, Springsteen went inside to check out an antiques shop in another hotel. "The clerk was about twenty years old and he started trembling when he saw it was Springsteen standing in front of him," Kerwinski recalls with a hearty laugh.

Landau also got out of the hotel and walked around in East Berlin. "I met some very interesting people and just got the sense that this was failing at a very basic level," he recalls. At one point he had a rather bizarre discussion with young FDJ members who claimed shows like "Dallas" were just Western propaganda deliberately and nefariously beamed deliberately into East Germany, to lure people to the West by giving them the false impression that every American was as wealthy as those portrayed on "Dallas." "There was a very specific party line from the various people we met," he says. "It felt very heavy and very alien to us."

Back at the Grand Hotel Berlin, there were often crowds of journalists and East German fans gathered outside, waiting to catch a glimpse, an autograph, or an interview with Springsteen. Dietrich Blume was thirty-three in 1988 and working as a doorman at the Grand Hotel Berlin. "There was a group of journalists milling around outside the day before the concert, and they wanted to know why Springsteen came to East Berlin," Blume recalls. "So he just went outside himself and told them: 'The people here have a right to hear good music, and that's why I'm here.' For me that was a really cool answer. He went out and told them the way it was. He told them he wasn't there for any reason, he wasn't going to let anyone use his name or let himself be used for any political purpose. He just told them that the people in East Germany had every right to hear good rock music."

Springsteen managed to maintain his down-to-earth style, although he was surely aware of the extraordinary circumstances. He later talked about his experiences in East Berlin, the chance to wander about and ride around before the show, in an interview with East German TV. The DDR2 network broadcast long segments of his concert on July 19 and during an intermission it aired the five-minute backstage interview with Springsteen.

In the interview Springsteen told the TV viewers that he had been in East Berlin before, for a day back in 1981, and ever since then had wanted to return to the city to play a concert for the people of East Germany. "It was something I had thought about for a long time," he said, adding he was very excited when East Germany quickly got back in touch with him and said "yes" to a concert. He could tell a lot had changed between from his first visit in 1981 to 1988. "It felt a little less gray to me this time than it did when I was here in '81. Even with the people on the street, there's a little more life, a little more color. I've been enjoying East Berlin very much so far," Springsteen told the TV reporter with a big smile. "It's great to be here. I'm glad we got the opportunity to come over . . . Everyone involved in the concert and all those who made it possible have been really fantastic, it's been wonderful."

Gerald Ponesky in 1988.

And then all of a sudden he runs across a young lady in East Germany who says 'No, it's not all quite that miserable all the time and we have our good moments too.'"

Günther remembers Springsteen being in particular curious about the lives of average East Germans. "He was really interested in all that, and eager to learn more. He guessed that we all had our good moments and bad moments. He asked me things like: what was the size of my apartment, if life in East Germany was easy, if I felt miserable living in a Communist country, and where I learned English, and how I was able to learn English in a country behind the Iron Curtain without ever traveling to an English-speaking country," she says. Springsteen seemed fascinated by the conditions in the GDR. "He asked me a lot of stuff about life as a single mother in East Germany, if it was difficult to manage working and being a mother at the same time, how I could work a full time job with a four-year-old son. I told him we had daycare centers. He asked me if I believed in what the authorities told us and what we read in the newspapers. I was frank with him and told him no, I didn't believe everything they told us, but I said I had a privileged position because I worked with foreign visitors all the time. I told him that because of that I knew quite well that what we were being told was lies."

Günther and Springsteen developed an open friendship and chatted candidly during their two days together. Springsteen even asked her at one point if she ever thought about fleeing from East Germany, a question that could have gotten her in serious trouble, had the Stasi or an unofficial East German informant been listening in. But she instinctively knew it was safe to talk to him and felt confident enough to give him an honest answer. "I told him at this stage, no, because the atmosphere was changing and we had the feeling that maybe something would change and that our lives would become easier," she recalls. "I told him our first dream was to be able to travel to other countries in the West. I told him I didn't really want to leave East Germany. I just wanted to travel more, have more freedom. By becoming an interpreter for English I'd hoped that I'd be able to travel. He didn't try to persuade me to go to the West or tell me that the West is better than the East. We talked about political issues, and he said that everything was far from okay in the United States too."

She also told Springsteen how she had studied abroad in the Soviet Union. "I had spent a year in Moscow. He found that extremely interesting. I remember he sort of envied me for that; it was like 'Oh wow, you've been to Russia for a whole year? How cool is that?'" Günther remembers their time together as an enlightening exchange of ideas. Springsteen gave her an autographed copy of his *Tunnel of Love* album and a tour sweatshirt, cherished souvenirs that she still has today.

Georg Kerwinski, Springsteen's Bavarian chauffeur and part-time translator, also spent a few hours driving around in East Berlin with him and Patti Scialfa before the concert. He remembers Springsteen and Scialfa were freshly in love and spent quite a bit of time locked in an embrace on the back seat of his Mercedes Benz. They came up for air enough, though, to see East Berlin and some of the more dilapidated parts of the city, far away from the central tourist boulevards that East Germany kept spruced up to show Westerners that life behind the Iron Curtain wasn't so bad. Kerwinski remembers Springsteen suddenly seeing a record shop on one East German street corner and telling him to pull over because he wanted to go in to have a look around.

"So we parked the car in front of the record shop and went in," Kerwinski says. "Bruce was just looking through the record racks, when all of a sudden the shop manager comes up to us. He didn't speak any English, so I had to tell the manager that Bruce was just looking. The manager then asked Bruce if he could step into his office in the back of the shop for a moment. I could tell Bruce didn't feel comfortable about that, so he asked me what the manager wanted. He said he just wanted to talk to him for a minute. So Bruce says, 'okay.' We get back there and the manager pulls out a Springsteen album of his own and asks him for an autograph. The album wasn't for sale in the shop, but he had a copy and just wanted an autograph. And he had to do it secretly so no one else in the shop would know he had a copy. It was all very strange."

Kerwinski said Springsteen also went for a long walk up and down Unter den Linden, the main east-west boulevard through

Previous page: An aerial view of the concert grounds and the enormous crowd taken from an East German police helicopter at about 5 p.m., or two hours before the concert began —the stage is in the foreground, left, in between the two giant sets of speakers.

Left: An aerial view of the concert entrance at Rennbahnstrasse several hours before the concert began.
Photos courtesy of Manfred Schmischke and the East Berlin police.

Chapter 7
STORMING THE GATES

Lying out there like a killer in the sun
Hey I know it's late, we can make it if we run
Oh Thunder Road, sit tight take hold, Thunder Road
Tonight we'll be free
　　　　　　　　　　　　　—Thunder Road

Before noon on July 19, 1988, the biggest concert crowd ever in East Germany began arriving at the venue in Weissensee, a residential district northeast of the center of East Berlin—more than seven hours before the start of the show. It was a warm mid-summer day, and temperatures would peak in the high 80s later that afternoon. There were already tens of thousands of fans waiting outside the no-frills venue when the gates were finally opened well ahead of schedule, at 2:10 p.m. The Stasi kept detailed reports of what was going on at the venue that day and noted that by 4 p.m. there were already 50,000 people present—a full three hours before the show.

The concert venue was spread out over a large swath of a fifty-five-acre park in Weissensee. Part of the tree-lined, grassy lot was originally used as a popular horse racetrack, called the *Trabrennbahn* (Harness-racing Track), between 1878 and 1912. The horse track was converted into a vast cycling venue after World War II, partly because horseracing was a sport that fell into disfavor under Communist East German rule when it was considered to be elitist. Gambling was also frowned upon in East Germany. A cycling track and stadium, called the Radrennbahn Weissensee, was built on the south side of the fifty-five-acre venue in 1954 with a capacity for 9,000 spectators. Even though many streets in

Berlin changed names several times during the last century, depending on whether the Kaiser, the Weimar Republic, the Nazis, the Communists, or a democratic government was in power, the street running in front of the grounds still kept the name Rennbahnstrasse (Race Track Street) throughout.

The concert grounds were about as basic as it gets—a giant featureless lot without modern amenities. There was only one main video screen set up about 80 yards from the stage, so that those in the back could at least see something. There were two slightly smaller video screens set up on both sides of the stage. They were relatively crude contraptions because it was all but impossible to get hold of state-of-the-art high-tech equipment in East Germany during the Cold War. So the local organizers improvised, doing the best they could to rig together the giant sound and video system. The stage, for example, had been built from sections of a steel bridge that had been under construction in another city. Because the video wall was so rudimentary, there was a split-second delay at first, between what was happening on stage and what appeared on the screen—a gap that greatly annoyed Springsteen, according to East German organizers. But by 1988 standards, it was still an amazing place, and there was nary a complaint about the lack of creature comforts. The people had come to experience Springsteen and didn't seem bothered about the rest.

As the afternoon turned into the early evening on July 19, 1988, the crowd kept growing larger, even though Springsteen and his band were not due to start playing until 7 p.m. The Stasi noted in its report, "At 6 p.m. the crowds are still filing into the rock concert area according to plan and without incident, aside from the occasional small jam of people. Based on current estimates, the number of people inside is about 70,000."

Countless tens of thousands of East Germans were streaming into East Berlin from all across the country, pouring into the capital from other East German cities such as Leipzig, Dresden, Magdeburg, Cottbus, Karl-Marx-Stadt, Neu Brandenburg, Potsdam, Halle, Erfurt, Jena, Suhl, Rostock, and Schwerin. They arrived in convoys of sputtering Trabants or in jam-packed train cars. Many tens of thousands skipped work or school that Tuesday to journey to East Berlin. An East German newspaper later reported that it was not only the biggest concert in East German history, but it also caused the biggest traffic jam the country had ever seen.

The roads around the concert area in the Weissensee district were so packed, in fact, and there was so much chaos on the streets, that even the driver of the car carrying Springsteen to the concert had trouble getting past a police roadblock. His chauffeur, Georg Kerwinski, was inching forward through the residential neighborhoods when he was stopped by an East German police officer and told to turn around and leave. "I tried to tell the East German cop that I couldn't turn around and go away because I had Bruce Springsteen in the car with me and he had to get to the concert that all these people were going to see," Kerwinski remembers with a laugh. "But the cop said he didn't care who was in the car." Kerwinski couldn't turn around even if he'd wanted to, but fortunately the roadblock was opened and the car carrying Springsteen was allowed to pass.

Many more people came than tickets were available. Only 160,000 tickets were printed for the concert. Of those, 60,000 were allocated to members or groups affiliated with the Communist youth organization, the FDJ. Another 20,000 tickets were given to the security organizations in Berlin to sell or distribute; 20,000 were set aside for concert-day ticket sales at ticket windows, and there were "another 20,000 tickets in reserve, in case the demand among youths was so great on the day of the show," the FDJ wrote in a report on the concert. Wise thinking, but not enough. The concert sold out quickly with tickets going for 20 East German marks, but far more people showed up without tickets, wanting to get in. The tickets were printed on ordinary pieces of paper and were not especially difficult to copy, even though photocopy machines in East Germany were carefully controlled and in limited supply. So thousands of counterfeit tickets were in circulation.

Even those without tickets joined the cheerful masses of young people headed for East Berlin, in the hope they might still get in. The streets around the Weissensee concert grounds were clogged all afternoon with the happy hordes of people wandering about, trying to make their way to the venue or get their hands on tickets. Ria Koch, who was a twenty-two-year-old medical student in 1988 and is an anesthesiologist now, says she didn't have a ticket for the concert but took a two-hour train ride from her home in Pasewalk with a friend to Berlin, with hopes of somehow getting in.

"When I heard Springsteen was coming to East Germany, I just knew I had to be there," she says. "We saw a line and got on it. East German people had a lot of experience standing in lines patiently. Nothing seemed to happen for ages, but then all of a sudden, someone said there weren't any tickets available anymore. After that, the whole line just started moving quickly toward the gates. It was like a giant herd, moving faster and faster. We ran for a while and then saw that a flimsy little stand for ticket sales had been overrun and in the spot where it was once were broken, splintered pieces of wood. It looked like the ticket sales stand just got run over and we were in. There was a second control point a little further in, but they only looked at our bags there; no one was asking for tickets by that point. It was amazing that we got through the gates and got in like that, without having tickets. It was an incredible dynamic that just materialized out of nowhere. A lot of us had come so far to see the concert and we were determined to get in. We just wanted to hear the music and after coming so far we weren't going to let anything stop us."

Many East Germans who were there said they had a sense that it might be their first and last chance to see anyone like Springsteen, and they were determined to savor the moment in case their country's opening proved ephemeral. Who knew how long the thaw would last in East Germany? Who knew if Gorbachev might be toppled by hardliners and these openings crushed as ruthlessly as those in East Germany in 1953, in Hungary in 1956, and in Czechoslovakia in 1968?

There were also 74 foreign correspondents there. One of them was Cherno Jobatey, who worked for the West German weekly *Die Zeit* and West Berlin's daily *Der Tagesspiegel* back in 1988. "I was a rookie reporter and just trying to break into the business," Jobatey recalls. "I was a bit of a pioneer in those days, because I was the only black journalist in Germany. I got lucky, and the newspaper sent me over." Jobatey, who is now one of Germany's leading TV news hosts, also remembers the long trek from the nearest East Berlin rail station to the concert grounds. There was something in the air that night. Couples were making out all over the place. I think a lot of people found new girlfriends or boyfriends that night. East Germans always had a certain reputation for being looser about sex. And there seemed to be a lot going on that night," Jobatey says.

The mood in Weissensee must have been similar to the sentiment at Woodstock, the legendary three-day festival for peace and music in upstate New York in August 1969. "The atmosphere was incredible, with a once-in-a-lifetime feeling. They didn't expect that many people to be there, but the place was packed," Jobatey says. "No one seemed to mind walking for hours to get there."

Birgit Walter, the journalist for *Berliner Zeitung*, remembers it was so crowded that she felt squeezed from all sides so she climbed up on top of a garbage can to get a better view and some space for a while. "It was a fantastic concert and the mood couldn't have been better," says Walter. Working for a newspaper in East Germany meant that she wasn't free to write everything she wanted about the concert because the Communist censors would have killed her story and that would have likely been the end of her journalism career. "I couldn't have written what I wanted to, I couldn't have written that most of the people at the concert wanted to go to the West, that the FDJ had organized the concert in an attempt to stop the exodus of young people applying for exit visas, I couldn't write that the concert was rather poorly organized by the FDJ and the people way in the back probably couldn't hear or see very much. I couldn't have written about all the discontent building in East Germany back then," she says. Walter was nevertheless content with the article she wrote for the newspaper, which focused on the music. "It was simply a great concert. It was an incredible experience for the people of East Germany to get to see this world star on their stage. There were so many people there. It turned into a community right then and there. People began thinking 'Hey, we've got power, maybe we can accomplish something.'"

East German organizers later admitted there were at least 200,000 and probably 300,000 people jammed into the meadow to watch. Some have estimated that as many as 500,000 people came. Roland Claus, who was also in charge of concert security for the FDJ, said it

The stage is being built.
Opposite page: The infamous Nicaragua sign.
Fotos: Herbert Schulze

was the biggest gathering ever in East Germany, with a crowd that was larger than the authorities dared to announce officially. "It was quite possibly at least 300,000 and maybe more," Claus says. "The number that was officially announced was actually smaller. But the real number couldn't be released because we simply didn't have permission to have that many people in there. We knew we'd have had problems if we said how many people were really there."

Claus says the pressure was so crushing that at some point the FDJ decided to order all the gates open, to just push down the fences and let everyone in, whether they had a ticket or not. According to Claus, the FDJ was worried about people getting hurt in a stampede and told the ushers to open up all the gates to prevent anyone from getting crushed. "We had a problem with the security fences," he says. "We had to just tip them over and let everyone in. If we had tried to keep it closed off, there could have been serious crowd-control problems and some people might have been seriously injured." Claus acknowledges that the decision to throw open the barriers was as extraordinary as it was controversial. He said the FDJ had to answer for itself to Communist Party leaders and argued that the FDJ had organized the concert and was thus responsible for what happened there at the grounds. "We were responsible for the event, the FDJ, and not the East German state, and not the Communist Party," Claus says, sounding proud of the defiant act even twenty-five years later. "The security people complained bitterly when we said, 'Open the gates'. But it was our decision. We told them we were responsible for the concert and it had been our call."

It was a remarkable act of capitulation inside Communist East Germany, a country where rules were taken seriously and regulations almost never so openly defied. East Germany was a totalitarian state, where the implicit threat of force always lurked just around the corner. Merely knocking down a barrier and running over it onto the concert grounds was a heady experience in its own right for many people there. Many who were at the concert later remembered in vivid detail their amazement at seeing the security gates trampled. It was something they had never seen before in East Germany—and wouldn't see again until November 9, 1989, when the Berlin Wall itself was broken open under similar pressure from an unruly-looking mass of people determined to break through the barrier.

Imke Handke, who was a lab assistant and twenty-three years old in 1988, remembers being surprised as she entered the concert grounds and saw the security fences being run over. She said the whole experience was surreal. "The fence got knocked down, and everyone just flooded in," she said. "It was all so amazing. You never saw anything like that happen in East Germany."

That was indeed a potent symbol for many East Germans in the year of 1988—to run over a barrier and not be shot at was a dream many shared. And sixteen months later, when the Berlin Wall did crack open, there was déjà vu of those scenes from Weissensee, when hundreds of thousands of East Germans poured through new openings in the Berlin Wall, such as at Bornholmer Bridge border crossing about three miles west of Weissensee, to see West Berlin. "Everything was chaos before the concert began," journalist Cherno Jobatey recalls. "There was no public order, and it smelled like a jungle. Then Springsteen started to play and he really rocked the place. Everyone went wild. The mood was really, really special. Everyone was like, 'I can't believe the number-one rock star in the world is really here, I can't believe this is really happening here in East Berlin.' Girls were fainting all over the place. I never saw so many fainted girls in my life. It was amazing. These guys were carrying all these girls who had fainted." The crowd was so tightly packed that people who fainted were simply lifted up over everyone's heads and passed over to the sidelines.

The Stasi seemed for the most part satisfied with the way the things were going and said the atmosphere was superb: "One person was injured near the entrance and taken to the hospital with a concussion. He was not in critical condition. There were also diplomats in attendance from Nicaragua and the United States of America."

Aboce: The fans are coming.
Below: A group from Thuringia.
Fotos: Herbert Schulze

Chapter 8
A Close Call

I wanna spit in the face of these Badlands
–Badlands

It was a warm summer evening when Springsteen took the stage in East Berlin on July 19, 1988. The sun was still shining and wouldn't set for hours during those never-ending Northern European summer evenings. "It's great to be in East Berlin," Springsteen shouted into the microphone, to an eruption of cheers. He whirled around to face the band and counted off the start of *Badlands*. After that came *Out in the Street, Boom, Boom, Adam Raised a Cain, All That Heaven Will Allow, The River, Cover me, Brilliant Disguise, The Promised Land, Spare Parts, War,* and *Born in the USA*. Everyone was standing. Some waved hand-stitched American flags—not an item you could normally find ready-made in East German shops. Others held up banners with the names of favorite songs. Everyone seemed to be having a great time.

Springsteen would sing thirty-two songs in East Berlin that evening and the choice to begin the concert with *Badlands* was inspiring. Anyone listening closely to the lyrics of the song, about a young man in trouble and angry at the world, might interpret *Badlands* as a provocative start to a show in a Communist country that was so out of touch with its younger generation. Springsteen was evidently still perturbed about the "Concert for Nicaragua" label that had been stamped next to his name on everyone's ticket, but was he really being so brash as to call East Germany "Badlands"? That's the message many people in the crowd understood.

"Lights out tonight, trouble in the heartland / Got a head-on collision, smashing in my guts man / I'm caught in a crossfire that

I don't understand," were some of the first lines to thunder out from the stage. "I don't give a damn for the same old played out scenes / I don't give a damn for just the in-betweens / Honey I want the heart, I want the soul, I want control right now."

Starting off with *Badlands* set the tone for the rest of the evening. A pulsating anthem written in 1977 for his 1978 *Darkness on the Edge of Town* album, *Badlands* was a staple on earlier Springsteen concert tours. But during "The Tunnel of Love Tour" in 1988 it had been largely dropped from the repertoire. He played it just nine times on the sixty-seven-stop "Tunnel of Love Express Tour." Springsteen had not opened any concerts that year with *Badlands*. Until he got to East Berlin.

Talk about a dream, try to make it real
You spend your life waiting for a moment that just don't come,
don't waste your time a-waiting...
Badlands you gotta live it every day

There were no restrictions placed on what songs Springsteen could play in East Germany. West German bands wanting to appear in the Communist country had not been as fortunate but had been subject to tight restrictions on what songs they were allowed to play, a nauseating intervention into artistic freedom. This heavy-handed police-state meddling had caused international incidents in the not-too-distant past.

Four years earlier, in 1984, a popular West German rock band from Cologne, called BAP, decided to pack up and leave East Germany rather than accept the decision of East German censors. The band abruptly cancelled a fourteen-concert tour on the eve of the first show in East Berlin because East German authorities tried to stop the group from playing one controversial song—"Deshalv spill' mer he" (Why We Playin' Here). BAP's leader, Wolfgang Niedecken, had written the lyrics in the band's signature Cologne dialect especially for their East German tour after comments he had made in an advance interview to East

German television were edited out of context and completely distorted. Niedecken, who had long been looking forward to the chance to play in East Germany, had explained that he was just as much against American Pershing missiles being stationed in West Germany, pointed east, as he was against the Soviet SS-20s being in East Germany, pointed west. Only the half of his message that was critical of the Pershing missiles was included in the East German TV broadcast.

Unintelligible for even most Germans outside of Cologne, the BAP song included lyrics that the East German censors would not allow, such as "He du da, und du, wann ist es hier so weit, dass man das Maul aufmachen darf, wenn man etwas sagen will?" ("Hey, you over there, you too, when do you think you'll be able to open your mouth here and say what you want?")—a direct challenge to the East German establishment and the lacking freedom of speech. BAP was told not to play the song in East Germany, but the band refused to accept that condition and scrapped the tour. Springsteen was aware that East German censors had made it difficult in 1984 for his friend Wolfgang Niedecken. But Springsteen did not face any restrictions himself, even though the lyrics to songs such as *Badlands, Chimes of Freedom,* and *Born to Run* could be interpreted as provocations to Communist East Germany.

"We knew that there were other groups that had played in East Berlin and that it was possible to perform there," Springsteen said in a 1988 interview with German Sat-1 TV network. "We didn't know the exact conditions and we didn't know what would happen. But you could feel that everything was getting a bit more relaxed compared to 1981. We had played West Berlin a bunch of times. We were over in East Berlin as tourists . . . We wanted to use the chance to play there in East Berlin."

Springsteen's *Badlands* includes a number of lines that could well have applied to conditions in Communist East Germany rather than, say, a troubled area in the United States. He also altered, ever so slightly, one of the refrains for the East Berlin crowd: He sang "Keep pushing 'til it's understood and these Badlands start treating us good" instead of "We'll keep pushing 'til it's understood and these Badlands start treating us good," subtly turning the statement into a command that could have raised eyebrows among the East German Communist leaders—if they had understood the message.

But it is unlikely that any East German Communist officials thought twice about the lyrics of *Badlands* or took it as a reference to their country. Nor did Communist authorities appear to notice or were they bothered by the subtle change in lyrics, which may have even been unintentional. East German TV nevertheless took the precautionary measure of slightly modifying, rather bizarrely, the title of *Badlands* to "A Badlands" on the tape-delayed broadcast of the concert—lest anyone conclude that Springsteen might have indeed been singing about East Germany. It's also quite likely that many East Germans, who were usually taught Russian as their first foreign language in school, might have entirely missed the meaning of what he was singing about, although many were singing along loudly to many of his songs.

It wasn't the first time Springsteen had used *Badlands* to make a point. He famously introduced the song to an audience in Tempe, Arizona, on November 5, 1980—the roiling night after Ronald Reagan was elected president—with a short but memorable and often-quoted speech: "I don't know what you guys think about what happened last night. But I think it's pretty frightening." Some Springsteen biographers have called the comment his first on-stage political statement. With *Badlands* lyrics like "I want to spit in the face of these Badlands," it doesn't require a great leap of the imagination to sense he was singing about Communist East Germany. Other lines from the song could be interpreted that way as well: "You spend your life waiting for a moment that just don't come—don't waste your time a-waiting . . . I believe in the faith that could save me / I believe in the hope and I pray that some day it will raise me above these Badlands."

Talk about a dream, try to make it real
You wake up in the night with a fear so real
Badlands you gotta live it every day
Let the broken hearts stand, as the price you've gotta pay

A Close Call

Keep pushing till it's understood. And these Badlands start treating us good
For the ones who had a notion, a notion deep inside
that it ain't no sin to be glad you're alive
I wanna find one face that ain't looking through me
I wanna find one place, I wanna spit in the face of these Badlands.

Badlands is neither the first nor only song Springsteen wrote with references to escape and freedom—ideas that held an intrinsic appeal for East Germans locked up behind the Wall. Even if the selection of *Badlands* to open the concert or the deeper meanings of the lyrics might not have been fully appreciated, the crowd still understood the point of what Springsteen was singing about: don't sell yourself short, believe in your dreams, and don't let fear get in the way of a desire to be free. It was a powerful message, indeed, to be delivering to a mass crowd of young people that evening in the middle of Communist East Berlin.

"Springsteen's mere presence in East Berlin was a tacit message to a lot of young East Germans, that more might be possible in their lifetime," says Jochen Staadt, the historian at the Free University of Berlin's East German research unit. "There was a trend in East Germany in the 1980s that encouraged people to dare to do more, that you could take a chance and get away with a bit more. The message that Springsteen delivered was 'Hey, this can happen here in East Germany too.' And it was powerful for 1988."

Springsteen was also carrying another, more direct message with him that evening. Just before the concert began, the issue of the "Concert for Nicaragua" slogan that was printed on the tickets had been on his mind, and he'd enlisted his West German interpreter and chauffeur, Georg Kerwinski, to help. Back at the East Berlin hotel and backstage, Springsteen had been telling everyone who would listen about why he wanted to play in East Berlin but just before the concert he needed Kewinski's language skills to help with a few lines in German, so he could explain it to the entire crowd.

"It was about five minutes before the show was set to begin and it all happened incredibly fast," Kerwinski recalls. "The band was already up on the stage. Someone from his security team came up to me and said: 'Bruce wants to talk to you.' So I went over to his dressing room. He was alone with a pen and piece of paper in his hands. It was literally just minutes before he went on. He told me he wanted to say something in German and wanted me to help him pronounce it. He said he wanted to tell the people he wasn't here for any political reason, that he came to play rock 'n' roll for the people of East Germany, in the hope that one day 'all the walls' would come down."

Kerwinski, who learned English while working as a DJ in London before moving to Munich, recalls that Springsteen was clearly upset about the Nicaragua spin the Communists had put on his concert. "My God, that bothered him and he wanted to make a statement because of what they printed on the tickets. He said he only wanted to play rock 'n' roll and that he hoped one day all the walls would be knocked down. So I translated those ideas into German. He wanted me to enunciate those ideas in a few German sentences, so I did that a couple of times, and he wrote it all down phonetically," Kerwinski says. "He wrote it all down, the way he heard it phonetically, then practiced by reading it back to me three or four times. It was important for him to get across the point that he came to East Berlin to play for them, without any political motive. He wasn't happy about the Nicaragua stuff and he wanted to make sure the people knew that was not the reason he came to play for them." Then Bruce went up on stage and started to play.

Ordinarily a cheerful man, Kerwinski might have been the only person at the concert who was not having a great time. Instead, he was backstage and worrying about the wisdom of being an accomplice for an American who planned to launch a verbal attack against the Berlin Wall from inside East Germany.

It was one thing to condemn the Berlin Wall from the safety of West Berlin—and just about every West German leader had spoken out against the Wall at one time or another, along with American presidents from John F. Kennedy to Ronald Reagan. Kennedy gave a historic speech in West Berlin after visiting the Berlin Wall on June 26, 1963—two years after the Wall was built—a speech mainly famous for the few lines he spoke in his American-accented German. But first he told a crowd of 450,000 people in West Berlin that the United States would continue to defend the city's liberty: "Freedom has many difficulties and democracy is not perfect, but we never have had to put up a wall to keep our people in." Kennedy went on to say: "Two thousand years ago the proudest boast was 'civis Romanus sum'—'I am a Roman citizen.' Today, in the world of freedom, the proudest boast is 'Ich bin ein Berliner' . . . All free men, wherever they may live, are citizens of Berlin and, therefore, as a free man, I take pride in the words 'Ich bin ein Berliner.'" The massive West Berlin crowd erupted in cheers, and Kennedy became a legend throughout Germany.

Twenty-four years later, on June 12, 1987, Reagan also spoke out against the Berlin Wall but to a much smaller crowd and under much different circumstances. In a speech to about 45,000 people in front of the Brandenburg Gate in West Berlin, Reagan used the Wall as a backdrop for his direct appeal to Gorbachev to tear down the Wall. "We welcome change and openness, for we believe that freedom and security go together, that the advance of human liberty can only strengthen the cause of world peace. There is one sign the Soviets can make that would be unmistakable, that would advance dramatically the cause of freedom and peace. General Secretary Gorbachev, if you seek peace, if you seek prosperity for the Soviet Union and Eastern Europe, if you seek liberalization, come here to this gate. Mr. Gorbachev, open this gate. Mr. Gorbachev, tear down this wall."

The last line of the speech was later called "the four most famous words of Ronald Reagan's Presidency," albeit as part of revisionist history in some conservative circles to attach greater significance to Reagan's legacy. As *Time* magazine noted years later, the media largely ignored the speech at the time: "For all its drama, the speech received relatively little media coverage." More attention was paid to the massive anti-Reagan protests in West Berlin during his trip when half a million West Berliners took to the streets to protest against his "Star Wars" defense policies.

So railing against the Wall from the West was hardly uncommon during the Cold War but didn't really accomplish much beyond making the people in the West feel good about themselves. In the East, the words were simply dismissed as Cold War rhetoric. In East Germany, the Wall was not officially referred to as the Wall ("Mauer") anyway because in their view "wall" was a loaded term used by Western propaganda to describe the barrier. Every self-respecting East German Communist Party member referred to the Wall by its politically correct term: "Antifaschistischer Schutzwall" (Anti-Fascist Protection Rampart). But it was another, thoroughly brazen thing to criticize the Berlin Wall in the middle of East Berlin during the Cold War, something no important Western visitor had dared in such a public way.

With Bruce Springsteen already on the East Berlin stage and making his way through the set list, Kerwinski was in a quandary about what to do with his knowledge that Springsteen was planning to speak out against the Berlin Wall. He knew that the Wall was locking up seventeen million East Germans as veritable prisoners in their own country. He also knew that many important people in West Berlin had called for the Wall to be torn down. But Kerwinski intrinsically knew that it was a completely different matter for Springsteen, a guest in the GDR, to bash the Wall from East Berlin when John F. Kennedy and Ronald Reagan made their famous anti-Wall speeches over in West Berlin. He was worried that the East German authorities might decide to pull the plug on the concert. No one knew how a disappointed and unruly crowd of 300,000 might react to an abrupt and premature ending of the biggest, most exciting rock concert that the Communist country had ever seen. And Kerwinski was clever enough to understand that it wouldn't take long to figure out that he was the one who had helped with the translation. There might be hell to pay. So he started chatting to people backstage about Springsteen's plan.

According to Kerwinski, he ended up telling his boss, West German concert manager Marcel Avram, about the looming anti-Wall speech. But, according to other accounts, word of the planned speech was already spreading backstage. In a place like East Germany, filled with networks of spies and unofficial informants, it did not take long for the Stasi to find out about Spring-

The Boss on stage in East Berlin . . .

. . . and it was a night that Bruce Springsteen would never forget. He sang his heart out and then spoke out against the Berlin Wall. Photos: Herbert Schulze.

steen's plan. "All of a sudden there was a lot of anxiety everywhere backstage," Kerwinski recalls.

Springsteen and his manager, Jon Landau, had talked before the concert about his doing a short speech from the stage. "Bruce and I had a chance to discuss the need for a statement and the general framework for it the night before," Landau says. Oblivious at first to the growing tension backstage, Landau had been savoring the concert atmosphere, spending time soaking up the moment on a walk through the crowd—although he had a hard time getting around because it was so tightly packed. Landau only got caught up in the commotion over the looming speech when he returned backstage. He was surprised that others had found out about it. "Marcel Avram comes running up to us and says, 'Are you trying to ruin me? Bruce is going to make a speech denouncing the Wall,'" Landau recalls. "I said, 'Marcel, hold on, how can you possibly know that?'" Landau adds, alluding to the widespread fear of East German spies and their ubiquitous eavesdropping devices. "I told him that Bruce had been sitting alone before the concert in an enclosed area backstage with only his translator," Landau says.

So how did so many people backstage know what Springsteen was going to say? Landau laughs. He pauses and takes a deep breath before pointing out that he had actually been planning to save that for his own memoirs. But he says he'll reveal the story now: "Okay, so it turned out that, for one reason or another, the driver, who was our regular driver in West Germany and acted as a translator, was talking to one of the many East German guests backstage, and I think in a sort of casual fashion he told someone what Bruce was planning to say. This word 'wall' just jumped out and everyone was really worked up about it because it was such a charged word at the time."

Since the word "walls" was causing so much angst backstage, Avram pleaded with Landau to have the speech dropped or at least get rid of that "W" word. Landau assured Avram that Springsteen was in East Berlin for a rock concert for East Germany—not to start an uprising—and that he would try to sort it all out. Thinking quickly as is his wont, Springsteen's right-hand man knew he'd need different word than "walls," lest that one-syllable term cause who-knows-what mayhem in East Berlin. He knew Springsteen well enough, after so many years of close collaboration and friendship, to understand the message Springsteen wanted to deliver and he knew that Springsteen would not want to cause problems for the scores of people who put the concert together for him. So Landau quickly came up with the term "barriers" as a substitute for "walls"—a somewhat less explosive word for the East German Communist sensibilities that would nevertheless get the same meaning across to the audience.

"The word 'walls' was such a charged term at the time," Landau says. "I decided that we didn't come here to have a confrontation with these particular officials. So I had the word translated into something other than 'walls.' The German word for 'barriers' is what we used. It just seemed like a prudent decision to substitute the word 'walls' with 'barriers.' I don't know if 'walls' would have caused problems. But it seemed that, under the circumstances, substituting the word was the right thing. That was my instinct. I had to act quickly, and that's what I thought. I just caught Bruce's attention on stage, and we made that one little change in what he would say."

Some may see that as a timid move but Landau knew Springsteen was interested in getting his message out without endangering the rest of the concert or sparking an international incident. He was, after all, inside East Berlin and this was still in the middle of the Cold War. "We weren't there in East Berlin to take an openly confrontational approach," Landau says. "We weren't there to protest to the government of East Germany. We were there to do a concert for those 160,000 people or 300,000 people or however many were there in East Berlin. I agreed to the word change because, in the big scheme of things, I was sure the audience would understand Bruce's deeper meaning."

Right after Landau caught his eye, Springsteen slipped away from the band for a moment and went down a narrow set of stairs in the middle of the stage, while his band played on. At the bottom of the stairs, where Springsteen had a pitcher of ice water set up on a small table for quick breaks between songs, he met

Landau and Kerwinski. Landau told him they had to change one word. "When I called Bruce over, while the band was playing, I actually said, 'Just make this change.' I don't remember him asking 'why?' or me telling him why. He just trusted it was the necessary thing to do." Kerwinski, the Bavarian driver, then shouted out the new word phonetically—drop "Mauern" (walls) and say "Barrieren" (barriers). Springsteen could barely hear Kerwinski and kept yelling, "What?"

"The band was playing and it was really loud," Kerwinski recalls. "We were screaming to each other, and I yelled, 'Drop the word 'Mauern,' walls. Don't say 'Mauern'! No walls! Bar-hee-AIR-en. Bar-hee-AIR-en. Barriers. We have to say 'barriers'. He shouted, 'What?' We had to scream because it was so loud. So I took the note out of his hand and crossed out 'Walls' and wrote 'Bar-hee-AIR-en.' That's a hard German word for Americans to pronounce."

Kerwinski said Springseen finally got the message, smiled, and gave a thumbs-up before climbing back up the stairs and onto the stage. It was just a few moments later when Springsteen pulled the piece of paper out of his pocket and delivered the speech:

Es ist schön in Ost-Berlin zu sein. Ich bin nicht für oder gegen eine Regierung. Ich bin gekommen, um Rock 'n' roll für euch zu spielen in der Hoffnung, dass eines Tages alle Barrieren abgerissen werden.

The English translation of what Springsteen said in German is: "It's great to be in East Berlin. I'm not for or against any government. I came here to play rock 'n' roll for you, in the hope that one day all barriers will be torn down."

Because it was so short, it may be one of the most under-appreciated anti-Wall speeches ever made. But considering that it was delivered inside East Germany, it probably did more to shake the Cold War barrier than all the anti-Wall speeches in West Berlin combined, by Kennedy in 1963, Reagan in 1987, and everyone else between. Springsteen was in East Berlin, being cheered by the biggest and most ecstatic concert crowd in the country's history, and he was speaking out in German against the Berlin Wall. He delivered the lines with an American accent that made it difficult for some of the people farther away from the stage or speakers to understand. But everyone close enough to the stage or the less-than-perfect East German loudspeakers understood what he meant.

"We all got the message, and it was electrifying," said Jörg Beneke, a thirty-four-year-old farmer in 1988, who drove halfway across East Germany with a friend that morning to see the concert. "Everyone knew exactly what he was talking about—tearing down the Wall. It was a nail in the coffin for East Germany. We had never heard anything like that from anyone inside East Germany. That was the moment some of us had been waiting a lifetime to hear. There had been other rock stars from the West who came and played and said, 'Hello East Berlin,' or something like that. But no one ever came to us and said he hoped the barriers would be torn down. No one ever showed that much courage. It was just incredible. We all felt locked up, and if we could have gotten over the Wall, many of us would have. He stands up there and then says he hopes the barriers would be torn down. Springsteen won everyone's heart over with that."

The crowd erupted in a deafening roar. It was short but powerful—an intoxicating moment in East Berlin. Springsteen smiled as the ovation rolled up and over the stage. He took a few steps back from the microphone as if he were being bowled over by the roar from the crowd. He gazed out at the sea of people with a proud look on his face as the applause only seemed to grow louder. They were already having the time of their lives, and then this American songwriter and rock star takes a moment to speak to them in their language, and tell them what no one else before had ever dared to say: that he hoped the Wall would be torn down.

Springsteen savored the reaction as the crowd celebrated their savior as much as themselves. He seemed extraordinarily pleased about delivering that message, in German, to an audience that he rightly sensed had a bottled-up craving for a free and better life.

Reinhard Heidemann, who was the East German government's point man for foreign entertainers at the East German Artist Agency, says he stood there in awe and also applauded Springsteen for his courage to speak out against the Wall—even though he was, of course, an official of the East German government that built and defended the Wall. Even though Springsteen did not use the word "Wall," "everyone knew what he meant," says Heidemann. "It was a bold thing to do. He knew exactly what he was doing. It was already a wonderful concert and that made the whole thing even more special."

Kerwinski was also impressed. "It was incredibly brave, what he did. I was thinking the East German authorities might pull the plug on the concert right then and there." But they didn't. And Springsteen was still beaming just seconds later as the crowd erupted again upon hearing the first chords of the next song—"Chimes of Freedom." They understood that message as well. They knew the title of the song that was starting. It was an emotional selection that amplified the message of his speech. "Chimes of Freedom," an expression of solidarity with people treated unjustly, was written by Bob Dylan. Even from the perspective of a quarter of a century later, Landau says he still gets chills when he recalls that moment when Springsteen spoke to the East Berlin crowd about his hopes that the Walls would be torn down. "The effect that the speech and then the song 'Chimes of Freedom' had on the audience was spectacular," he says. "It was a moment none of us will ever forget." With the hindsight of twenty-five years, Landau says, "Bruce just wanted to make it clear to the crowd that he was not a tool of the East German government, or any government. Whether the word was 'wall' or 'barrier' was ultimately irrelevant, and if using the latter would keep things a bit calmer with the authorities—that was all right. We didn't over to get involved in some kind of international incident. The public would understand as we know they did."

The East Germans who organized the concert weren't smiling. Despite the relief that the term "walls" had been replaced with "barriers," they were still worried about possible backlash from East German Communist government hardliners over Springsteen's speech, which even in its milder form was still unambiguously critical of the Berlin Wall.

Gerald Ponesky says that a top Communist Party official named Egon Krenz, who was in charge of the FDJ at the time,

had stopped by to see the concert for himself. Ponesky and other organizers backstage had also learned that Springsteen was planning to talk about the Wall and were alarmed. Krenz, who was fifty-one in 1988, happened to arrive at the concert just before Springsteen's speech. The FDJ leader arrived at 8:10 p.m., according to a Stasi report on the concert, and left just thirty minutes later, at 8:40 p.m.

"We heard through the grapevine that Springsteen wanted to say something like 'The Wall has to come down,' and if he had said that, it would have been the end of everything for all of us," Ponesky says. "Who knows what would have happened? But we all knew we'd have never been able to work again in the music industry in East Germany and we'd have had problems because of that for the rest of our lives." Ponesky recalls that, even after Landau's intervention, he and other East Germans who had worked to make the concert happen were still nervous about possible repercussions over Springsteen's use of the word "barriers"—a clear reference to the Berlin Wall.

But fortunately for Ponesky, and his team, Krenz had been there at the right moment and heard what Springsteen said. The FDJ leader would become known to the world just fourteen months later, when he succeeded Erich Honecker—but his reforms turned out to be too little and too late. Krenz ruled for just seven weeks before being deposed himself. Ponesky recalls Krenz being asked what he thought of Springsteen's "barriers" speech. Krenz said it was fine with him. "We thought we'd still have a problem, but Krenz was standing in the VIP area. Krenz said something like 'We're all against barriers,' and we were all relieved after that."

Kerwinski, the chatty West German chauffeur, remembers the atmosphere backstage remaining tense right up to the address because no one knew exactly when Springsteen was going to speak out against the Wall, and they were afraid they might be too late with the switch. Landau admits it was a close call. How close? "About ten minutes," he says, still somewhat taken aback by all the drama of the moment. When it was suggested that it could make for great scene in feature film some day, Laundau laughed and said: "I've thought of that too!" He believes the East German officials did not overreact to Springsteen's speech, possibly because the initial protests over the Nicaragua billing the day before sent notice to East German officials that they were unhappy by the attempts to surreptitiously enlist Springsteen to their cause. "The East German officials were accommodating and perhaps because they had no real choice once Bruce hit the stage they didn't overreact when Bruce made his statement," Landau says.

After *Chimes of Freedom*, the concert continued with *Paradise by the C, She's the One, You Can Look (But You Better Not Touch), I'm a Coward (When it Comes to Love), I'm on Fire, Downbound Train*, and then *Dancing in the Dark*.

In the middle of "Dancing in the Dark," Springsteen began searching the crowd for a dance partner—as he often did during that song. He spotted Heike Bernhard, an attractive seventeen-year-old brunette who had arrived six hours before the concert began and was standing in the crowd near the stage. He pointed to her and waved enthusiastically for her to come up. Bernhard rushed toward the stage and was lifted up with help from people around her. Then Springsteen reached out his hand to lead her up on stage. "It was an overwhelming experience," Bernhard said in an interview with the East German youth magazine *Neues Leben*. The popular magazine duly noted she had a boyfriend who was not at the concert because he was a soldier serving at a remote outpost in the East German army. "I didn't notice the crowd or anything at all anymore. We just started moving to the music. It was like a dream." Bernhard also told the East German magazine that her boyfriend later spotted her dancing on the stage with Springsteen, on a delayed East German TV broadcast of the concert.

After a few minutes of dancing together, the song ended, Springsteen embraced Bernhard, and then stepped back to join the crowd in applauding her dancing. They held up their hands together, turned to wave to the crowd, and took a bow together. It looked like Bernhard was close to fainting, trembling for a few seconds before Springsteen steadied her and then helped her back down into the crowd.

The next day, Heike Bernhard went to Springsteen's hotel with a girlfriend to try to meet the rock star and get his autograph. She

told *Neues Leben* she got an autographed photo from him that read, "For Heike, thanks for the dance."

Bernhard did not give any further interviews after that for twenty-five years. But the most envied women in the history of East Germany finally broke her silence in a 2013 documentary film about Springsteen's 1988 concert, jointly produced by the public broadcasting networks arte, MDR and RBB. Bernhard, now forty-two, explained in the documentary *Kalter Krieg der Konzerte—Wie der Boss den Osten rockte* how she got to the lines outside the concert grounds early that day and made a friendly bet with her friends while waiting outside that she would somehow manage to get on the stage with Springsteen. When he started singing *Dancing in the Dark*, he looked out as he sang "I'm searching for my baby." And Heike Bernhard says she instinctively just started pushing her way forward toward the stage. She was surprised to see him staring and waving at her to come up on the stage. She got lifted on the stage and the crowd went wild. "When you're up there on the stage and look down, you can't see any single person any more. The only thing I saw was this unbelievable mass of people cheering and applauding like mad. The only thing I could think of was 'okay, now you've got to dance'. It was like my brain just went on auto pilot."

In his position at the Artist Agency, Reinhard Heidemann says he'd seen a lot of international musicians parade through East Germany before but there had never been anything like Springsteen. "It was the best concert ever," recalls Heidemann, who was thirty-nine at the time. "Springsteen was a great entertainer, he gave a great show, and created a wonderful atmosphere. He was relaxed and was totally engaged with the crowd. He even pulled that young woman out of the crowd for a dance. Everything went well. It was an incredible atmosphere."

The Stasi seemed for the most part content with the way the concert was proceeding. An entry in the East German state security agency's log of the concert some two hours after Springsteen started to play reads: "9:30 p.m.—the rock concert continues without incident. The atmosphere in the crowd is very good." The report later reads: "State security was not in any way compromised. A total of 800 people collapsed during the concert, including about 110 due to alcohol consumption."

It had long since grown dark in Berlin as the concert extended well into its fourth hour. But Springsteen kept playing, following *Dancing in the Dark* with *Because the Night, Light of Day, Hungry Heart, Glory Days, Can't Help Falling in Love, Bobby Jean, Cadillac Ranch, Tenth Avenue Freeze-out, Sweet Soul Music, Twist and Shout,* and finally, *Havin' a Party.*

Springsteen played for nearly four hours that evening, in another one of his trademark marathon concerts that totaled thirty-two songs and two encores. When the East German DDR2 TV network reporter asked him earlier during the intermission interview backstage about why his concerts last so long, Springsteen smiled and laughed before answering: "Well, once you get all the equipment set up, you might as well just stay for a while. I just enjoy it. I always did. I used to play in clubs in the United States when I was sixteen and we'd play for four or five hours. Usually I get paid so well. So once I get up there, I should do a little work." The reporter also asked him how many of his songs are based on his own experiences, to which Springsteen replied: "I'd say maybe half and half. I think all of it comes out of the emotional experience. Even in the songs where the details are different from your own life, it comes up out of your emotional life so in some ways you've experienced them yourself. To write well about something you have to feel it at some time. I look at my job as sometimes I'll assume a character in a song and try to walk in another man's shoes for a while and see what his life is like and hopefully bring up a little compassion for the guy next door. That's the idea anyway."

After about five minutes and once the questions started to meander toward the effusive and political, Springsteen glanced down at his watch and told the East German TV reporter that he had to get back on stage: "Hey, I gotta go do my job now." But the East German journalist hurled one last question his way, as Springsteen was already backpedaling from the camera. The journalist asked, like a good East German Communist would, about the deeper meaning of the song *War* that Bruce had just played. Many East Germans felt like they were in constant danger of being attacked by the West during the Cold War, and the East German regime liked to portray itself as one of the world's most pacifist nations. Springsteen's *War* was seen in some circles as a protest against the Reagan Administration's policies in Nicaragua and Central America. So a Westerner like Springsteen criticizing war fit perfectly into the East German Weltanschauung—and with the Nicaragua theme the concert organizers had tried to impose. Springsteen was already a step or two away when he heard the question, but he stopped, paused briefly, and smiled into the camera, saying: "It's a great song. It says it all. 'War', you know, 'what's it good for? Nothin!'"

After the concert Springsteen went briefly to a reception hosted by the FDJ. Accompanied by Patti Scialfa, he listened dutifully to a speech from a local leader of the FDJ who effusively praised Springsteen for coming to East Berlin and for his stirring performance. Conny Günther remembers it being a rather stiff gathering with about 20 FDJ leaders all eager to toast him. "I was feeling sorry for him because he was having to endure all this after the concert but he was a good sport about it all and thanked them for having him," Günther says. "At one point I was afraid they were going to start calling him 'Comrade Springsteen' in one of the speeches because they were so over the top. I would have translated that as 'Mr. Springsteen' but fortunately they didn't go that far. They all just loved the concert and kept telling him that. He didn't hang around too long and was gone after about twenty or thirty minutes."

Springsteen and Scialfa were back at the Grand Hotel Berlin and watched a rebroadcast of the concert on East German TV together with Landau. They listened while the East German reporter repeatedly tried in vain to get Springsteen to saying something political or critical about the United States. "To try to lighten things up, Bruce just said 'Well you gotta remember the pay is pretty good'," Landau says. "But they didn't translate or subtitle Bruce's answer into German. That East Germany might somehow feel threatened by him joking about the fact that that pay for a rock star is pretty good said a lot about the insecurity of the East German government at that point."

It was jam-packed at the concert grounds. Photos: Herbert Schulze

Below: A fan who has passed out is carried away. Photos: Herbert Schulze

Chapter 9
POWER TO THE PEOPLE

Well, the night's busted open
These two lanes will take us anywhere,
We got one last chance to make it real,
To trade in these wings on some wheels
  —Thunder Road

Many East Germans who saw Springsteen that evening report it had a powerful effect on their lives. Even a quarter century later, many vividly recall the details and the atmosphere. The concert created a new sense of community, an intangible bonding of a generation in East Germany that was eager and ready to unshackle itself after decades of totalitarian control. A smile instantly flashes across the face of those who are asked about the concert in Weissensee and more than a few describe it as a turning point in their lives, a liberating moment on an evening when they felt it was all right to begin dreaming about a brighter future.

"It was all so insane, there were so many people, and the mood was so good," says Gabi Gärtner, a sales clerk who went to the concert as a nineteen-year-old with her boyfriend, Ralf Wurzel. He had never seen an American before. The atmosphere was magic; everyone seemed intoxicated by the moment and the energy of the music so that they were able to forget for a few hours where they really were. "We were standing near a video screen, and near the end of the concert a pipe burst open, with some kind of coolant in it, and it started spraying muck on everyone standing nearby," Wurzel recalls. "We were already kind of dirty because it had rained before the concert and the grass was wet and muddy. But we were all in such a great mood that no one was bothered after getting sprayed.

That's how happy we all were." Yvonne Wagner was twenty years old when she went to the concert with friends and was also curious to see an American in person for the first time. "I can still remember when he sang 'Born in the USA' and we all sang along with him," the Berlin secretary says, smiling at the memory of 300,000 East Germans shouting the refrain in unison with an American rock star. "We sang it loud and with so much enthusiasm. Incredible. It was so fantastic. None of us had ever experienced anything like that at a concert before. Most of us didn't really understand the lyrics, but it sounded good and it was just so much fun to sing 'Born in the USA'—even if we were all born in the GDR."

For anyone raised in East Germany and taught in school that the United States was the "imperialist" arch enemy of the Soviet Union and the GDR, it certainly felt odd to be singing those lyrics together with Springsteen that evening. Often misunderstood, *Born in the USA* is anything but a patriotic rallying cry, but rather an elegiac piece about the Vietnam War, a song about a troubled American veteran who can't find a job when he returns home. The East German crowd loved the song and the lyrics—especially because it felt somehow verboten to be shouting *Born in the USA* in the middle of East Germany. It must have sent shivers down the spines of Communist Party officials to see hundreds of thousands of East Germans joyfully singing along with Springsteen, many waving hand-made American flags.

Herbert Schulze was a photographer assigned to cover the concert for the East German magazine *Neues Leben* and had spent several days ahead of the show watching the giant stage, sound system and video walls being put together—everything was on an enormous scale. During the concert he was stationed right in front of the stage and was, like many others, overwhelmed at the size and energy of the crowd. But what really struck the then thirty-six-year-old photographer was the outpouring of pro-America sentiment—in the heart of East Germany. It was bizarre and so unusual, he says. Everywhere he looked out into the crowd he saw hand-made American flags, pro-America slogans, red-white-and-blue banners or signs. "That was something I'd never seen in East Germany before," says Schulze. "Normally anything pro-America like that was totally verboten! You couldn't just go out on the street with an American flag in your hand because you'd be in big trouble if you tried to do anything like that. Everyone knew you couldn't do a stunt like that in the GDR. America was the class enemy and yet there at the concert were all these people holding up American flags and banners. It was incredible. That all these people were holding up American symbols and not being punished for it or even worried about getting in trouble was a totally new experience for me."

In good spirits himself at the concert, Springsteen told East German TV reporters in that short but famous interview during the intermission that he was baffled that the crowd knew the lyrics to so many of his songs. "It's fantastic, incredible," he said of the Berlin crowd. "I was surprised how many people seemed to know the music. A lot of people were out there singing along, a lot of people seemed to know the words. They had banners out there with the titles of the songs written on them. It's great, just fantastic."

Ria Koch, the twenty-two-year-old medical student in the crowd who crashed the gate, remembers she knew the lyrics to all the songs on *Born in the USA* because she had gotten her hands on that album a few years earlier. "I knew the lyrics because I had listened to it so much at home," she says. "I was able to sing along with so many of the songs because I knew most of them by heart. It was a great experience and such a wonderful atmosphere." But Koch, who got to the venue in the early afternoon and had a spot not far from the stage, also remembers it getting increasingly congested in the hours before the show began. The feeling of claustrophobia became too much for some people nearby, she recalls. "It was getting more and more cramped," says Koch, who is five feet, ten inches tall. She said she and her friend were tall enough to see over the heads of most of those around them. But she remembers a shorter woman standing nearby who was becoming increasingly distraught by the pressure. "We could see she was having problems and getting scared. Suddenly she said something like 'I don't think I'm going to make it.' So we all picked her up and lifted her on our shoulders. She started feeling better again after a while." The Stasi later reported that eighty people had fainted and needed treatment.

Jörg Beneke, the thirty-four-year-old farmer, arrived at the concert grounds shortly after 4 p.m. "From today's perspective, you just can't imagine what it was like," he says. "We stood there for six hours without anything to eat or drink; we weren't able to go to the bathroom because we just couldn't move anywhere. I still don't know how I managed to hold out that long. Whenever someone passed out, they were simply lifted up in the air and passed to the back above everyone's heads. It was so jammed that sometimes you'd get swept up off your feet and carried five to ten yards to the left or right without your feet ever touching the ground. But there was no violence. It was all completely peaceful."

Beneke remembers being astonished by the size and energy of the crowd. "We'd never seen anything like it." He is convinced that the concert changed the country. "It was all so surreal for us. We all saw how wonderful something like that could be. There were 300,000 young people there, having this great big party, and we got a whiff of the freedom that we had never had before. Everyone saw what could be possible on that night, and after that we all wanted more." Not long ago Beneke, who is from a town north of Berlin, met his son's girlfriend near Leipzig for the first time. "Her mother had been to the Springsteen concert too, and right away we had something to talk about for hours. For anyone who was there, talking about the concert always makes you smile."

Birgit Walter, the journalist for *Berliner Zeitung*, agrees the Springsteen concert marked the beginning of the end for Communist East Germany. "The time was ripe for a change," she says. "The FDJ thought they could do something for the younger generations to make them happy. But at the concert everyone could see what a farce that was. The discontent just kept growing and people didn't want to be part of that system any more. It was a last attempt to give the people a reason to want to stay but it had the opposite effect because everyone noticed what we were being cheated from having when we saw Springsteen perform. Everyone started thinking about what it would be like to have concerts like that all the time and no longer be at the mercy of a few people at the top."

Herbert Schulze, the photojournalist, says that there was already a sense of change in the sentiment in East Germany before Springsteen came to East Berlin. There was a longing for reform and people were simply fed up with being controlled and suppressed. "The mood in the country was already changing a bit at that point and in last two years of East Germany people were getting away with more than anyone had thought possible before. The state couldn't really control the masses of people the way they once did. Springsteen came and stepped right into all that. He was like a symbol of freedom for a lot of people." Schulze still proudly owns the scores of the color photographs he shot at the concert and of the work that went into setting up the concert ground, proudly displaying the images as historical artifacts.

"The Springsteen concert was completely different from anything we had ever experienced in East Germany and you could feel that the mood was changing after it," said Andreas Dubois, a twenty-seven-year-old scientist at the time, who got to Weissensee early enough to get a spot to stand not far from the stage. "For the first time there was a world-class star who came to play for us, the crowd was totally into what he was doing on the stage, it was unbelievably packed and Springsteen succeeded in taking the crowd with him where he wanted to take us. Everyone could feel that he wanted to make sure everyone was having a great time, that everyone saw a great concert and that everyone went home feeling better. There was this underlying sentiment in the crowd that night that people didn't want to live behind a Wall anymore. It was gradually dawning on everyone between about twenty and thirty years old that things couldn't just continue in East Germany the way they had been going. Something had to change. And then Springsteen came and his concert fit right into all that."

For many East Germans, it was the most intense experience of their lives. Gärtner says it was a spectacular moment for the GDR, but also one that made people yearn even more for the freedom Springsteen symbolized. "After the concert we all had to walk home, because the streets were closed off to public transportation and cars," Gärtner recalls. "There were so many people everywhere. It was a giant crowd that went waltzing through the streets of East Berlin that night. It felt like a great big demonstration or something. Everyone had such high hopes all of a sudden. It was all so euphoric."

It would be the last summer that Gärtner and Wurzel would spend in the east together. Wurzel fled East Germany to West Germany through a new opening in the Iron Curtain between Hungary and Austria just ten months later, in May 1989, and Gärtner followed him out of East Germany five months after that, in October 1989—one month before the Wall collapsed. "We were sick and tired of the confinement, of being told what we could and couldn't do, and of all the rules constantly being imposed upon us, and not being able to speak our minds freely," says Wurzel, who now lives in the same eastern Berlin neighborhood he left in 1989 when he fled East Germany. "We all saw the Springsteen concert as a sign the East German leaders were giving up a bit. They knew that they had to do a lot more to keep the young people happy. But it wasn't enough. It didn't work. We just wanted more freedom after that."

Other East Germans who were at the concert can still fondly recall that extraordinary moment of East German history and agree that things in East Germany were never quite the same again. For many it was the first time they were part of a large crowd, because Communist authorities upheld a strict ban on demonstrations or gatherings of more than a handful of people. Many remember a new feeling of empowerment with new collective might—precisely the sort of uprising the East German rulers feared.

The Communists had long worried that assemblies of even small groups of demonstrators could lead to larger movements that would cause problems for the totalitarian state. So for most of the 300,000 people at the Springsteen concert that evening, it was the biggest free and unrestricted gathering they had ever been part of. "There were large official gatherings in East Germany, but we all had to be carted somewhere in buses to go to those things," says Koch. "This was completely different. We were there because we wanted to be there, not because we had to be there. We weren't sent there. We were there of our own free will. It was a wonderful concert. The atmosphere was incredible. It wasn't like anything we'd ever seen before." Jana von Rautenberg, who was twenty-three and working for East German TV in 1988, was also awed by the size and energy of the crowd. She remembers the whole city of East Berlin was abuzz on the day of the concert. "Everyone was in such a good mood because we knew Springsteen was coming," she recalls. "It was unreal that he was really going to play for us in East Germany; it was just all so hard to fathom. It seemed a bit like something from another planet had arrived."

Beate Kriese was only nineteen and journeyed three hours from a northeastern corner of the country to become part of the biggest gathering she had ever seen. "We knew only a little bit about Springsteen but couldn't really believe that such a big international star from the West was actually coming to play for us in East Germany. We were thrilled to have the chance to see a live concert by such an important artist. It gave the country a splash of international flair that we'd never seen before."

Lutz Rösler, a forty-three-year-old teacher in a trade school near Teltow, south of East Berlin, got a ticket to the show from the FDJ, a gesture of gratitude for the work he did as a soccer referee in a local youth league. "The atmosphere was beyond words," recalls Rösler. "Big stars like that didn't just drop into East Germany every day, you know. For the few hours he was here playing for us, there was no East Germany or West Germany anymore, there was no Berlin Wall, there was no Cold War. It felt like all the borders were gone." He wasn't a Springsteen fan beforehand but knew many of his students were, so he didn't dare mention the concert before traveling to East Berlin. "The next morning I must have looked a bit tired. The kids at school asked me where I'd been, and I said, 'I went to see Bruce.' They couldn't believe it. They were really upset about that; they had wanted to go and then had to hear their teacher talking about being there." Rösler was definitely a fan by the end of the show.

Imke Handke saw things at the 1988 concert that she had never seen before in East Germany—a massive gathering of people and mass adulation for an American in the middle of a country where school children were raised to fear Americans as villains who wanted to destroy their homes with nuclear weapons. "I was all so unreal," she says. Both Handke and Rösler went to see Springsteen perform again twenty-four years later, when he played to a sell-out crowd of 58,000 at the Olympic Stadium in unified Berlin.

Matthias Beck believes the concert changed his life. Beck, a carpenter who was twenty-two in 1988, also became a lifelong Springsteen fan that evening. He took a three-hour train ride from Zittau to East Berlin, even though he didn't have a concert ticket. Like many of his countrymen, he felt stifled in East Germany, and he thought the Springsteen concert would be a chance to get a glimpse of another world. "I came up to East Berlin in the hope I'd somehow get in to the concert," recalls Beck, who added he still gets goose bumps whenever he thinks about that evening in 1988. "The atmosphere was just insane. The crowd was the biggest mass of people I'd ever seen anywhere. Everyone just got swept in, with or without a ticket." The crowd was packed so tightly near the stage that after a while his legs went wobbly. "If my legs gave out on me, I probably would have been held in place standing, because we were all packed in together so tightly." He said he eventually grew so fatigued from all that pressure that he moved toward the back.

Oliver Michalsky was a student in 1988, aged twenty-four. He was surprised to find out a big Western star like Springsteen would really be coming to East Berlin. There had been a several Western acts in East Berlin that year, part of the FDJ's belated efforts. But none were as prominent as Springsteen. Michalsky, who is now the deputy editor of *Die Welt* newspaper, adds that no one in East Germany took any notice of the FDJ's attempt to put a Communist spin on the concert with the Nicaragua labeling; he still proudly owns his "Konzert für Nikaragua" ticket stub.

"It didn't surprise any of us that the FDJ had tried to sell the concert as an 'act of solidarity for Nicaragua,'" Michalsky says. "But that was totally irrelevant for most of us. We just wanted to see Springsteen. It was a giant mass of people making their way there, and then when we got there we saw this huge field packed with an incredible number of people. It was a great experience, even though the sound quality was abysmal. I was hundreds of yards away from the stage at first and could hardly hear anything. After pushing forward for about an hour, I managed to get close enough to a few of the loudspeakers halfway to the stage, to at least hear his music. My friend gave up and left. But I stayed until the end."

Like many others who entered the Weissensee concert grounds, Michalsky said he remembers seeing the security gates knocked

The concert went on until deep into the night. Fotos: Herbert Schulze

over as the masses streamed in. "I'd never seen anything like that," he recalls. "Seeing fences run over like that was the opposite of what we were used to in East Germany. Normally, the GDR was a place of order, of tight security everywhere. Trampled fences just wasn't part of the way of life." As he stepped over the fallen barricades, Michalsky did not think at the time that he might have been witnessing the beginning of the end of the GDR. His mind was attuned to more pragmatic issues. "The only thing I thought was 'Oh, gee, I guess I didn't have to buy a ticket after all.'"

Michalsky had also seen the Bob Dylan concert nine months earlier and was left disappointed by the lack of interest the American songwriter had shown for his audience. Springsteen, by contrast, had been a completely different experience. "He played his heart out in Weissensee," Michalsky says. He gave them a sweat-drenched performance and earned the deep admiration of the East German crowd. "He was totally engaged with the audience," he remembers. "Dylan had been really disappointing. He didn't say a word of welcome at the start and didn't even say goodbye at the end. Not a word. He just did his thing, sang some songs, and took off. It was a real let down, because Dylan had been someone a lot of people in East Germany looked up to. But the atmosphere was totally sterile. Springsteen was different. He spoke to the audience and he went all out for us. It was a great show."

Dietrich Blume, the doorman from the Grand Hotel Berlin where Springsteen and the band were staying, got his hands on a concert ticket from someone in the crew. Blume remembers it as a brilliant concert and was in awe over the way Springsteen went all out for the audience. "The music said it all. It had an overwhelming effect on the people. The music was so powerful. It was really impressive. It was an emotional night for all of us who were lucky enough to be there. Look at me," he adds with a smile. "Even twenty-five years later, I still get worked up thinking about that night. Everyone who was there still talks about it."

As impressive as Springsteen was on stage, Blume remembers him as a down-to-earth guest at the hotel. "He was totally unpretentious. He was down here in the lobby a lot, just hanging out with other band members or with his girlfriend. He wasn't stuck up at all, just a normal guy. On the morning after the concert, I saw him over here in the lobby and went over to say 'thanks for the great show.' I told him that the people in East Germany could tell he was up there singing for all those who don't really have anyone standing up for them in their corner. I told him I thought that was the great part of the show and why the resonance was so overwhelming. Then he started thanking me for thanking him for the great concert. Can you believe it? He actually started thanking me! It was unreal."

For many East Germans, the concert was without doubt an important steppingstone on the path toward the revolution in the fall of 1989. But others remember it simply as a great concert that had precious little or nothing to do with the political and social upheaval that followed. "Looking back, you can definitely see it as a sort piece of the mosaic to what happened a year later, with the Wall falling," says Handke. "People were hungry for change, and we were willing to do something about it—at least in our minds at that point. At the time, we all felt locked up in East Germany. There were so many restrictions on what we could do, what we could think about, what we could say. The government probably thought the Springsteen concert might serve as a bit of a 'safety valve' to let off some steam, so that they'd be able to stay in power for a long time to come. But it only made us hungrier for more."

Beck says the hunger for freedom in East Germany had always been there, just beneath the surface, even long before Springsteen. "This desire was always on our mind," he says. The young carpenter had been in the crowd at the Wall in East Berlin, trying to listen to the West Berlin concerts a year earlier, in 1987, when East German security forces beat people with truncheons. Beck remembers that for many other East Germans, the Springsteen concert was the turning point in their lives and changed their views on Communism and changed their views on their country and the conditions they were forced to live under. Years later, after Germany reunified, Beck was at a Western German concert and met a West German man about his same age. The man started to weep with envy when Beck mentioned he had seen Springsteen live at the 1988 concert.

The situation in East Germany was clearly worsening in the latter half of the 1980s. Frustration with the status quo was growing, and the number of people requesting exit visas to officially leave was rising, even though they would have to wait long periods for the visas and endure humiliations during those idled periods. "There was a lot of dissatisfaction at the time, the people were discontent and wanted to live in freedom," Beck said. "Things were in flux in East Germany in the late 'eighties." Georg Kerwinski, the driver from Bavaria, had seen a lot of Springsteen concerts before being a witness to what happened in East Berlin on July 19, 1988. He also says it changed his life and believes it changed the course of history. "The ground was heaving," he says. "It wasn't planned, and no one expected anything like that to happen. But it was an omen of change for the GDR. It was definitely the beginning of the end."

Conny Günther, the East German woman from the Artist Agency assigned to assist Springsteen those two days, calls it a fantastic concert that fed the movement for reform. "We were hungry for change," she remembers. "I don't know if everyone heard his speech or understood it, but they did understand what he was trying to express by coming to them. The mood in East Germany changed after the concert. People went home in great spirits from the concert, and it lasted. People talked about the concert for weeks. Here was this big star from the West, from America, and he's here and interested in our fate. He talks about how one day there won't be any barriers. You felt so much stronger after being part of a mass crowd like that. We started losing our fears. The East German authorities brought Springsteen and these other Western bands in to let off steam. But it all backfired on them. It didn't let off steam. It got young people thinking more about freedom."

Landau, Springsteen's manager and friend, says the band was overwhelmed by the size of the crowd, and Springsteen was awed by the experience. He struggled to push his way through the crowd for about half an hour, to get to the outer edge of where people were standing on the field. He had never seen anything like that before or after. "It was an enormous experience for us all," says Landau. "It was a great experience for the band to be onstage and interact with such a large audience. It was something that none of us who were there are ever going to forget. The electricity in that space, the big field, was just so spectacular. I can remember there was this big smile on Bruce's face. Put yourself in his shoes: to be able to go to a different culture, a different system, and unite people at some deep level and pull an audience together like that and create a shared experience. It was just an amazing thing." Springsteen has also talked about the East Berlin experience. Many years later, when he returned to reunited Berlin in 2012 for a concert in Olympic Stadium on his "Wrecking Ball Tour," he spotted a fan near the stage, holding up a sign that read simply, "Ostberlin 1988." There were many thousands of people in attendance that evening who had also been at the 1988 concert. Springsteen took a break between songs and reached out for the poster as a souvenir. He smiled at the memory and reflected back on that concert. "Once in a while you play a place, you play a show that ends up staying inside of you, living with you for the rest of your life. East Berlin in 1988 was certainly one of them."

Springsteen came back to Berlin again and again after 1988, a newly reunited city that was as fond of him as he was of it. In 1993 he played in West Berlin's Waldbühne. In 1995 he was back to again in what had become one of his favorite cities in the world to do a rare music video of *Hungry Heart*. He set up in a Café in Prenzlauer Berg, then called Café Eckstein, now Café Butter. Always a perfectionist, he and the band, that included BAP lead singer Wolfgang Niedecken joining in, played it about ten times before he was satisfied. Because the equipment was all set up and Springsteen enjoyed performing, they played a few more songs for the growing crowd that was gathering inside and outside the café for the improbable, spontaneous and free concert. In the "Hungry Heart"-video itself, Springsteen is seen driving around in Berlin in a convertible sports car and through the Brandenburg Gate that was opened when the Wall fell six years earlier. He also drives past a preserved half-mile long section of the Berlin Wall known as the "East Side Gallery" and just stares at the remnants of the Berlin Wall for moment. He is surely pleased that the graffiti-covered slabs of the Berlin Wall are now only a tourist attraction and no longer divide Berlin and the world. Quite possibly, Springsteen is thinking back to that magical evening in 1988 and wondering if what happened in Weissensee might have been a catalyst for historic events that soon followed.

Chapter 10
Tears in His Eyes

Well everybody's got a hunger, a hunger they can't resist
There's so much that you want, you deserve much more than this
Well, if dreams came true, aw, wouldn't that be nice
But this ain't no dream, we're living all through the night
You want it? You take it, you, you pay the price
                                  —Prove It All Night

Nothing was ever the same again in Communist East Germany. Less than sixteen months after the concert, the Berlin Wall fell. And gradually, the country known as the Deutsche Demokratische Republik, or the German Democratic Republic, disappeared.

Springsteen's manager, Jon Landau, says "the Boss" certainly did not go to East Berlin with the intention of changing the world, but after seeing the giant crowd of people out there that summer evening and the hunger in their eyes, he quickly realized that it was definitely more than just another rock concert. It was a show that changed East Germany—and also changed Springsteen. "Bruce walked off the stage after the concert, and we said—you know just personally to each other—that we had a feeling a big change was coming in East Germany because of the amount of explosiveness out there and all the energy," Landau says. "We just had a feeling about it. When he and I talked afterwards, we both sort of felt the system over here, these people, these people in the crowd, our audience, they were just busting out. They were just ready for change. You could feel that things were going to need to change."

Landau says they had not been in East Berlin long enough to understand everything that was going on at the dawn of that pivotal sixteen-month period leading up to the fall of the Berlin Wall. But they all felt the remarkable energy from the crowd as well as a powerful hunger for change. "We could feel that the ability to control that energy by those people in charge was slipping away very quickly and it turned out that it was." Whether the Springsteen concert helped let the genie out of the bottle is for historians to decide, Landau reckons. But everyone in the band had a sense that something special happened on that field that night. "If we made some little contribution to all that, that's fabulous. And if the concert did help shake things up in East Germany, that's great. While we were thrilled as so many were when the Wall came down, we've never presumed to believe that we were part of that. If others believe we played some role in it, so much the better. But, truly, that is for others to judge. As for me, it felt like we were in the right place, at the right time, doing the right thing with the right audience. It remains a thrilling and satisfying moment for all of us, even after all these years."

Springsteen felt the yearning for freedom from East Germans, Landau says. They sensed change was in the air. "We saw that, and you felt that in the crowd," he recalls. "You couldn't be at that show and not feel that hope for a change. We could certainly feel the energy there. The spirit with which we went into East Berlin was 'Hey, this is an adventure, something different.' It felt timely, but we weren't going over there in an arrogant state of mind or like we were evangelists for the West. That was not the case at all. But on the other hand I wouldn't minimize the outcome. The result was explosive. It was the magnitude of the whole thing."

It was more than just the size of the crowd—whether it was 160,000 of 300,000 or half a million. There were also millions more who watched excerpts on East German television or listened to it on radio station DT64 or on tape-delayed broadcasts. Beyond the record-breaking size of the crowd, what made the concert so extraordinary was the energy between Springsteen and the audience, an unforgettable bond forged amid the excitement of the moment at such an important juncture in the history of East Germany. "Springsteen created this incredible vibe that everyone took home with them," says Cherno Jobatey, the young journalist who wrote *Born in the DDR*, a long feature article for the West German newspaper *Die ZEIT* about Springsteen's eagerness to play in East Germany. "After the concert, there was this sort of hush of quiet everywhere, but everyone was smiling. They were all like 'Wow, I've seen it.' It was like their soul had been touched or something. There were a lot of happy people that night."

It may have been a too-little, too-late attempt by the East German FDJ youth organization to appease or even tranquilize the younger generation, a half-hearted effort to quell their lust for greater freedoms. But it all went badly wrong for the Communist East German leaders. The concert ended up having the opposite effect and serving as a powerful agent for change.

Springsteen brought together 300,000 young East Germans starved for change and gave them a new sense of community—and a taste of the energy, the excitement, and the empowerment of a large gathering. The concert obviously inspired many East Germans to take a new look at their suppressed lives and only fueled their desire for a better future in a freer world. The Springsteen concert in East Berlin shook East Germany in ways far more deeply than the Woodstock festival that rocked earlier generations in the United States, in August 1969. Woodstock, sometimes referred to as pivotal moment in U.S. music history, was "three days of peace & music," when thirty-two bands played on a soggy field in upstate New York. Woodstock also ended up turning into a free concert when 500,000 people showed up at the gates.

East Berlin left its mark on Springsteen, too. He was deeply moved by the concert there and has called it one of the most memorable he ever played. Kerwinski, who translated Springsteen's message to the East German audience, has seen a lot of rock stars in his day but he says he will never forget the way Springsteen and the band members were overwhelmed by the thunderous applause following Bruce's anti-Wall speech. "They were really, truly stirred," he says. "Bruce and everyone in the band, they all had tears in their eyes."

Years later, in an interview with the German Sat-1 TV network for a broadcast marking the tenth anniversary of the 1988 Weissensee concert, Springsteen said that playing in East Berlin had been an extraordinary experience indeed for him and his whole band. "That was the biggest concert we ever did. It was different from all our other concerts. When you play a place where something is happening, where something's in the air, you're influenced by that," Springsteen said. "Suddenly, everything's completely different than the hundreds of evenings before. That's what my music should be all about." Springsteen also said he would never forget the sight of so many East Germans holding up their homemade American flags and banners. "I can still remember some of those faces in the crowd. The people were there with these American flags they had stitched together from pieces of cloth. It was very moving for me and it was emotional." Even though Springsteen generally avoids comparisons about his concerts, he said the East Berlin crowd brought out the best in him and his band. "I think it was our best concert in a long time," he said.

The East Berlin concert was even still very much on his mind nearly a quarter of a century later, in May 2012, when Springsteen played at the sold-out Olympic Stadium in Berlin during his "Wrecking Ball Tour." Springsteen opened the concert by playing a song called "When I Leave Berlin," a special tribute to the 1988 concert in East Berlin. "When I leave Berlin" was his own adaptation of a 1973 song by English guitarist, singer, and songwriter Wizz Jones. "This is something we learned just for you," Springsteen said before nodding his head briefly, as if to say "thank you, Berlin" for giving him the memory of being part of one of the greatest and most important rock concerts ever anywhere. The lyrics included "When morning comes and I'll leave Berlin, my mind is turning, my heart is yearning, for you." He adapted the song with a few new lines of his own such as "I'm here today, but the Wall is open and gone are the soldiers and guns," and "I know for certain I'm a free man when I leave Berlin."

So what effect did the Springsteen concert have on the developments that swept across East Germany later in 1988 and in 1989? A number of historians and music history scholars believe that the concert had a lasting and profound impact on East Germany, although there are some who are cautious about drawing a direct link to the collapse of the Berlin Wall sixteen months later.

"Springsteen's concert and speech certainly contributed in a larger sense to the events leading up to the fall of the Wall," says Gerd Dietrich, a history professor at Berlin's Humboldt University. He said the FDJ hoped young people might be more content with their situation if they got to the chance to see someone like Springsteen. "But it didn't work out as planned. It made people only more eager for more and for change. The organizers wanted to demonstrate their openness. But Springsteen aroused a greater interest in the West. It showed people how locked up they really were."

Thomas Wilke, a lecturer at the Martin Luther University in Halle-Wittenberg, has written extensively about the impact of rock and pop music in East Germany. He is certain that the mood in East Germany was different after the Springsteen concert and that it seemed as if the whole country was either at the concert, watched it on TV, listened to it on the radio, or was otherwise aware of it. He was only thirteen years old at the time but remembers reading about the concert and hearing about it through the media. He says the concert rattled the East German Communists so much that they never again gave permission for another big concert like that, although FDJ leaders like Claus had been hoping to book the Irish rock band U2 to do a pan-Berlin concert a year later in the summer of 1989.

"The Springsteen concert changed quite a bit in East Germany," says Wilke. "It was the biggest concert ever in East Germany and it was a topic of discussion for quite some time afterwards. Even though one has to be careful about cause and effect, there was clearly a different feeling and a different sentiment in East Germany after that concert." Jochen Staadt was persona non grata in East Germany because he wrote critically as he tracked the country's development from Berlin's Free University on the west side of the Wall. He agrees that the East German government's plan to let Springsteen in to mollify younger generations didn't work and thinks it even made the situation more unstable and untenable. "The Springsteen concert was a contributing factor to the collapse of the East German regime and the Berlin Wall falling," Staadt says unequivocally. "People who saw the concert live or on TV thought . . . 'If that can happen here now, maybe more will happen here later.'"

In the summer of 1988, no one was expecting or could have dreamed of the fall of the Berlin Wall just a little more than a year later. Neither did Staadt. But it was clear that there were changes sweeping across the country, and Springsteen's concert was an important catalyst. "That the country had to open itself up for someone like Springsteen was already a signal that it was having problems. And when someone like Springsteen plays in front of such an enormous crowd of young East Germans, it must have been a clear signal to those in power: 'Hey, we want a different way of life here.' It also sent a strong message to people all over East Germany."

From the arrival of Gorbachev in 1985 until the moment the Berlin Wall opened in 1989, Staadt says he was frequently surprised by the way the East German regime was being pushed forward to accept developments it had previously resisted—like its gradually relaxed stance toward Western rock music. The Springsteen concert fit right into that trend and, at the same time, took it to the next level. "What was new was that so many people were there, they were sharing a common feeling together at the concert, and they were doing what they wanted," he says. The concert was more than a rock show. It galvanized East Germans and encouraged many to be bolder in expressing their desires—it gave the people there a newfound sense of their power. "It was amazing that the East German regime had let all that happen."

Just over a year later, in September 1989, hundreds of thousands of East Germans began taking to the streets, demanding changes of the East German government in regular demonstrations that would have been absolutely inconceivable before the Springsteen concert. The official East German TV networks dutifully ignored the mass rallies in East Germany, but Western TV stations broadcast reports on the demonstrations. "People in the GDR were no longer quite as surprised to see so many people massed together. I think it's because they had gained self-confidence after the Springsteen concert, and that had an effect on the mood," Staadt says.

The mass demonstrations in many East German cities began about thirteen months after the Springsteen concert, on September 4, 1989. Until then it had been unthinkable to stage a mass protest against the Communist regime. But throughout September

1989, the marches began gaining momentum in cities like Leipzig, Dresden, Magdeburg, Rostock, and Potsdam. The rallies were held under the slogan "Wir sind das Volk" (We are the people). It was the building pressure from these peaceful anti-government protests that led directly to the collapse of Honecker's regime in October 1989, and ultimately the opening of the Berlin Wall a month later.

Craig Werner, a professor of music and cultural history at the University of Wisconsin–Madison, says it is easy to overlook the links between popular culture and changes in society; he believes the Springsteen concert had a clear effect on the course of history in East Germany. "Music can play a significant role in supporting a movement that is already there," says Werner, who is also a member of the Nominating Committee of the Rock and Roll Hall of Fame and has taught university courses on the influence of Springsteen's music. "And East Berlin in 1988 was exactly the kind of place where music could support and inspire people who are active or potentially active. Springsteen's concert by itself didn't cause the Berlin Wall to fall. But it was a significant piece of the mix. East Berlin at that time was a place where Springsteen had an important role to play."

Matthias Döpfner, chief executive of the Axel Springer publishing company and an erstwhile music critic, wrote a review of Springsteen's Frankfurt show in the *Frankfurter Allgemeine Zeitung* just days before the East Berlin concert. In a recent interview in his office overlooking the strip where the Berlin Wall once stood, Döpfner says he is a firm believer in the power of rock 'n' roll and can well imagine Springsteen's concert in Weissensee had a revolutionary effect on East Germans. "I truly believe that, at the right moment and the right place, an artist can do more to change the world than lots of clever speeches by smart people supported with a myriad of logical arguments."

Springsteen has spoken about the East Berlin concert and the impact it had. He was moved by the sheer size of the massive crowd and he was touched by many of the faces in the crowd and their "I-can't-really-believe-this-is-really-happening-here" smiles. Those ear-to-ear grins on the faces of those young East Germans can be seen on the East German TV broadcast of the concert, still available on the Internet. They have smiles of disbelief on their faces, uncannily similar to the grins East Germans had on their faces sixteen months later when the Berlin Wall burst open and hundreds of thousands of East Germans crossed over into West Berlin for the first time in their lives—also captured by TV cameras from around the world.

Springsteen was braced for a different kind of experience playing behind the Iron Curtain. He wasn't really sure what to expect from the audience in the country where people were denied simple freedoms, but he was eager to soak up the atmosphere, to feed off it, and possibly to learn something about himself in East Berlin.

"It was so completely different," Springsteen said in an interview with German television ten years after the Weissensee concert. "You know, we grow accustomed to freedom. And it's completely natural that at some point you take freedom for granted. That's probably just all part of the luxury of having freedom. But I'm not sure it has to be like that. When we were playing in East Berlin, they didn't have that. And that also fundamentally influenced that concert, what you're playing for and what it's all about. An artist is sometimes at his or her best when you have to go up against something. If everything's too easy, work becomes just a theory. It can also be powerful, but when it gets practical and real, it's also a different thing for the audience. That's exciting, immediate and intense."

Springsteen came back to Berlin time and again. In 1995 he played again in Berlin, at the ICC in West Berlin. In 1999 he was back for two shows at the Wühlheide in southeastern Berlin, in 2002 he played indoors at the Velodrome cycling track, in 2005 at the ICC and then in 2012 at the Olympic Stadium.

But that special concert in East Berlin remains on Springsteen's mind even today. In November 2012, during the U.S. Presidential election campaign, he spoke of some of the "galvanizing moments", like playing in East Berlin, that he and his wife Patti have experienced while traveling the world: "We played in East Berlin one year before the fall of the Berlin Wall and we were with Amnesty International a year before the release of Nelson Mandela and the end of apartheid," he said. "Those were days when you could feel the winds of change moving and the world shifting beneath your feet."

Above left: Cindy Opitz, an American who traveled to East Berlin to catch the sound of Western pop music. Above right: Medical student Ria Koch was amazed how easy it was to get in without a ticket. Below left: Andreas Dubois got close because he arrived hours early. Below right: Historian Jochen Staadt in 1988, shows off his drumming skills.

Above, left: Oliver Michalsky, who struggled to hear the music because the crowd was so large, shows off the official paper of the East German Socialist party, Neues Deutschland. *Above, right: Jörg Beneke, an East German farmer, drove for hours to see Springsteen. Below: Conny Rudat, Springsteen's translator, sitting on the stage before the concert (left), and with the American singer Tom Petty (right).*

Postscript

Because the night belongs to us
—Because the Night

In the sixteen months since the first edition of *Rocking the Wall* was published in June 2013, many more eyewitnesses to the concert, Springsteen fans, former American soldiers stationed in West Berlin at the time, newspaper reporters, radio journalists, college students from around the world and even members of Springsteen's very own band have written or called me to learn more about the concert or share their memories of what happened on that magical evening on July 19, 1988. I was invited to dozens of talks about the book with its thought-provoking thesis in Germany and the United States and also on a trip generously sponsored by the American Council on Germany and even got a thank you note from German Chancellor Angela Merkel, to whom I gave a copy of the book after she told one radio interviewer that she was a Springsteen fan. I also did scores of media interviews about the concert and the book with journalists from newspapers, magazines and radio stations from Brazil to Berlin, Ireland to Italy, China to Canada, Mexico to Minnesota and Sweden to Sydney. But what moved me more than anything else was a letter from Bill Halpin.

Halpin was a U.S. officer stationed in West Berlin in 1988 and saw first hand what an effect Springsteen had had on the East Germans. Halpin felt the earth shake beneath his feet in East Berlin that evening watching Springsteen and told his fellow officers two days later that he believed the Berlin Wall would be gone within eighteen months – a highly radical idea at the time. Halpin got dragged over to East Berlin for the concert after his teenage daughters found out about it and persuaded him to come with them across the Berlin Wall to see it. Halpin said he felt like he was probably the only American officer in the middle of Communist East Berlin watching Springsteen that evening but he said he felt strangely at home in a sea of handmade American flags even though he said he saw the Volkspolizei (People's Police) and Stasi security police arrested some of those bolder East Germans who unfurled their makeshift U.S. flags.

"The crowd was riddled with Stasi and Vopos. We watched as they hauled off young people who displayed any 'highly illegal' U.S. symbols or paraphernalia—T-shirts, hats with U.S flag insignia. I saw more U.S. symbols that night in East Berlin than one would expect to see in Washington, DC, on the Fourth of July: It was amazing! Bruce was well received, but when he sang *Born in the U.S.A.*, the place erupted. It was a distinct moment of American pride—U.S. flags were waving everywhere in the crowd! The following Thursday morning, I attended the weekly USCOB/U.S. Mission staff meeting. As was the routine, I was the first staff member to report on issues and/or incidents affecting West Berlin vis-à-vis Soviet and/or East German political-military actions.

"My briefing was short and to the point: 'The Berlin Wall will fall within eighteen months without firing a shot.' As you might imagine, some around the table snickered, others were incredulous. So I explained what I'd witnessed at the Bruce Springsteen concert, knowing full well that the genie 'was not going back into the bottle.'" Halpin was still in West Berlin sixteen months later when the Berlin Wall burst open—a full two months sooner than he had predicted. "I'm happy to learn that my impression of that extraordinary night in East Berlin was shared by so many of the East Germans. One thing I always wondered about was the origin of all those U.S. flags. Now I know they were all handmade – incredible!"

The winds of change blowing through East Germany picked up in the months that followed the Springsteen concert. Just six weeks later, in September 1988, there were demonstrations for more freedom of speech in a high school in the Pankow district of East Berlin, near the Weissensee concert venue. In early October 1988, a West Berlin singer, Rio Reiser, gave a concert to an enthusiastic East

Berlin audience and sang his song *Der Traum ist aus* (The dream is over). The East Berliners shouted the refrain "Dieses Land ist es nicht" (This isn't the country) with a frighteningly powerful gusto that made the arena's walls tremble. Another month later and four months after the Springsteen concert, in November 1988, there were widespread protests against the East German government's decision to abruptly ban the Soviet *Sputnik* magazine.

And a few months after that, the Iron Curtain did finally begin to crack open, in May 1989, when Hungary took down the barbed-wire fences along its border with Austria. In September 1989, a year after the Springsteen concert, the first opposition movement in East Germany, "Neues Forum" (New Forum) was created—even though it quickly outlawed by the Communist government. September 1989 also saw the emergence of those huge, weekly, and peaceful rallies demonstrating for reforms in Leipzig, East Berlin and many other cities throughout the country. Communist leader Erich Honecker's stern reign collapsed in October 1989 without a single shot being fired, and just one month later the Berlin Wall fell, on November 9, 1989—marking the symbolic end of the Cold War. East Germany's first free, multiparty elections were held in March 1990, and on October 3, 1990, East Germany merged with West Germany, becoming part of the Federal Republic of Germany.

Talk to those who were there in July 1988, and they'll tell you the German Democratic Republic was a different place after Springsteen came. Younger and not-so-young generations, whose whole lives until then had been tightly controlled and closely monitored by a Communist dictatorship, were suddenly less afraid to stand up to the authorities and make their voices heard. The roots of that East German revolution can clearly be traced to extraordinary moments like Springsteen's rock concert. It helped many young East Germans find their voice, showed them what they could be and fed into a rising tide of disillusionment in Communist East Germany that turned into a broader rebellion—fueled by a yearning for freedom. And that's what brought down the Berlin Wall.

The original official poster for the Bruce Springsteen concert in 1988, designed for the Freie Deutsche Jugend, the FDJ. After the objections against the "Nikaragua"-label, it was not widely distributed.

Get the T-shirt at:
www.cafepress.com/
berlinica

Select Bibliography

Books, TV Programs, Archives, and Newspaper Stories

Alterman, Eric. *It Ain't No Sin to Be Glad You're Alive: The Promise of Bruce Springsteen*, New York, Little, Brown, 1999.
Carlin, Peter. *Bruce.* New York: Simon & Schuster, 2012.
Gerth, Steffen. "Legendäre Konzerte: Stars and Stripes über Ost-Berlin," *Der Spiegel*, July 19, 2008.
Humphries, Patrick and Hunt, Chris. *Blinded by the Light.* New York: H. Holt, 1986.
Jobatey, Cherno. "Born in the DDR," *Die Zeit*, July 29, 1988.
Marsh, Dave. *Bruce Springsteen on Tour: 1968–2006.* New York: Bloomsbury, 2006.
Marsh, Dave. *Bruce Springsteen: Two Hearts: The Definitive Biography 1972–2003.* New York: Routledge, 2003.
Marsh, Dave. *Glory Days: Bruce Springsteen in the 1980s.* New York: Pantheon Books, 1987.
Remnick, David. "We Are Alive. Bruce Springsteen at sixty-two," *The New Yorker*, July 30, 2012.
Sawyers, June Skinner and Scorsese, Martin. *Racing in the Street: The Bruce Springsteen Reader.* New York: Penguin Books, 2004
"Bruce Springsteen: Das ganz private Interview" (German TV interview), SAT1 network, December 15, 1988.
East German television network DDR2.
West German television network ARD.
German Commission Preserving Records of the East German State Security (Stasi archives) at Karl Liebknecht-Strasse 31-33 in Berlin, Germany.

Bibliography

Interviews with the Author

Beck, Matthias. May 30, 2012.
Beneke, Joerg. September 7, 2012.
Blume, Dietrich. September 13, 2012.
Claus, Roland. February 27, 2012.
Döpfner, Matthias. October 17, 2012.
Günther, Conny. August 17, 2012.
Handke, Imke. May 30, 2012.
Heidemann, Reinhard. February 20, 2013.
Jobatey, Cherno. October 13, 2012.
Kerwinski, Georg. August 15, 2012.
Koch, Ria. February 20, 2012.
Kreise, Beate. May 30, 2012.
Landau, Jon. March 9, 2012. March 20, 2013, April 10, 2013
Michalsky, Oliver. September 7, 2012.
Murphy, Philip. August 30, 2012.
Ponesky, Gerald. August 20, 2012.
Roesler, Lutz. May 30, 2012.
Schwenkow, Peter. September 29, 2012.
Staadt, Jochen. September 25, 2012.
Werner, Craig. August 23, 2012.
Wilke, Thomas. February 21, 2013.

Selected Websites

http://www.youtube.com/watch?v=yN7G6SdINS0
CBS Evening News feature on Springsteen in 1984.

http://www.youtube.com/watch?v=5V6eW8l0RyM
MTV interview with Bruce Springsteen in 1984

http://www.youtube.com/watch?v=O_jsVWQG77o
West German TV report on violence at Brandenburg Gate over David Bowie concert in 1987.

http://brucespringsteen.net/news/2012/bruce-thanks-germany-with-premiere-of-when-i-leave-berlin
Springsteen's 2012 tribute to the 1988 East Berlin concert with the song "When I leave Berlin"

http://vimeo.com/43189694
Another video if the 2012 tribute to the 1988 East Berlin concert with the song "When I leave Berlin"

http://brucespringsteen.net/news/2012/bruces-speech-from-madison-wi)
Bruce Springsteen's November 5, 2012 speech punting for Barack Obama from Madison, WI.

Photo Credits

Courtesy of Jörg Beneke: 150 above, right
Courtesy of Danny Clinch: 62, above
Courtesy of Ria Koch: 149 above, right
Courtesy of Chris Drukker: 12
Courtesy of Ilka Dubois: 149 below, left
Courtesy of Oliver Michalsky: 150 above, left
Courtesy of Cindy Opitz; 149, above, left
Courtesy Gerald Ponesky: 8, 46, 62 below, 85, 155, 159
Courtesy of Conny Rudat-Günther: 18 below, 74, 82, 150 below
Courtesy of Manfred Schmischke / East Berlin Police: 88-89, 90
Herbert Schulze: 18 above, 31, 96-97, 100, 109-110, 116-117, 120-121, 125-126, 135-136, cover picture
Eva C. Schweitzer: 32, cover picture
Courtesy of Jochen Staadt: 149 below, right

HERBERT SCHULZE, born 1950 in Berlin, was the official photographer of the Springsteen concert, and also one of the most well-known music photographers in East Germany. Today, he still has his photo studio in Berlin, where he lives with his wife.

A photo signed by Springsteen, thanking East Germans for the great concert in the East Berlin daily Berliner Zeitung. *"Thanks for a fantastic night in East Berlin we will always remember! Bruce Springsteen. P.S. Hope to see you again soon."*

 **PRESENTS**

2010–2014 PROGRAM

AVAILABLE AT

WWW.BERLINICA.COM

WWW.AMAZON.COM

WWW.BARNESANDNOBLE.COM

Michael Brettin / Peter Kroh
BERLIN 1945. WW II: PHOTOS OF THE AFTERMATH

Hardcover, 218 pp., $29.95
ISBN: 978-1-935902-03-4
Softcover, 218 pp., $19.95
ISBN: 978-1-935902-02-7

Erik Kirschbaum
BURNING BEETHOVEN

Softcover, 176 pp., $13.95
ISBN: 978-1-935902-85-0
Ebook: $7.95
ISBN: 978-1-935902-85-7

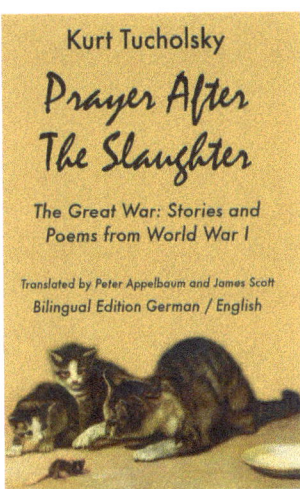

Kurt Tucholsky
POEMS FROM WW I

Softcover, 112 pp., $11.95
ISBN: 978-1-935902-28-7
Ebook: 978-1-935902-24-9

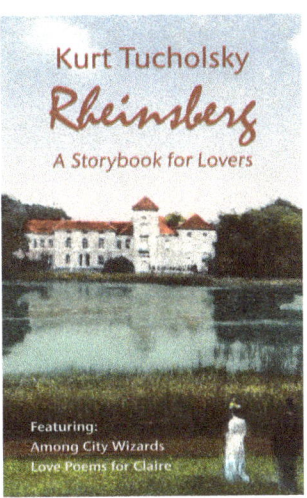

Kurt Tucholsky
RHEINSBERG

Hardcover, 96 pp. $14.95
ISBN: 978-1-935902-25-6
Softvover: 978-1-935902-27-0

Kurt Tucholsky
BERLIN! BERLIN!

Hardcover, 198 pp., $23.95
ISBN: 978-1-935902-21-8
Softcover, 198 pp., $15.95
ISBN: 978-1-935902-23-2

Mark Twain
A TRAMP IN BERLIN

Hardcover, 176 pp., $22.95
ISBN: 978-1-935902-92-8
Softcover, 176 pp., $14.95
ISBN: 978-1-935902-93-5

Andreas Nachama, Julius Schoeps, Hermann Simon
JEWS IN BERLIN
Softcover, 310 pp., $23.95
ISBN: 978-1-935902-60-7

Holly-Jane Rahlens
WALLFLOWER
Softcover, 150 pp., $11.95
ISBN: 978-1-935902-70-6
Ebook: 978-1-935902-71-3

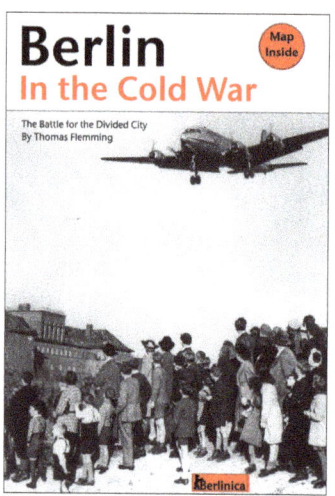

Thomas Flemming
BERLIN IN THE COLD WAR
Softcover, 90 pp., $9.95
ISBN: 978-1-935902-80-5
Ebook: 978-1-935902-81-2

Monika Maertens
BERLIN FOR FREE
Softcover, 104 pp., $10.95
ISBN: 978-1-935902-40-9
Ebook: 978-1-935902-41-7

Lothar Heinke
**WINGS OF DESIRE
ANGELS OF BERLIN**

Hardcover, 102 pp., $25.95
ISBN: 978-1-935902-14-0

Softcover, 102 pp., $16.95
ISBN: 978-1-935902-18-8

Available also in German

Rose Marie Donhauser
**THE BERLIN COOKBOOK
TRADITIONAL RECIPES
AND NOURISHING STORIES**

Hardcover, 96 pp., $24.95
ISBN: 978-1-935902-51-5
Softcover, 96 pp., $19.95
ISBN: 978-1-935902-50-8

Michael Cramer
**THE BERLIN
WALL TODAY
REMNANTS,
RUINS,
REMEMBRANCES**

Softcover, 86 pp.
$15.95
ISBN:
978-1-935902-102

German Edition
ISBN:
978-1-935902-119

Ebook: 978-1-935902-12-6

Adrienne Haan
BERLIN, MON AMOUR

*Music CD, 1 disc
in English or German.*

*Music from the 1920s,
by Bert Brecht, Kurt Weil,
and Friedrich Hollaender*

48 minutes; retail $15.95

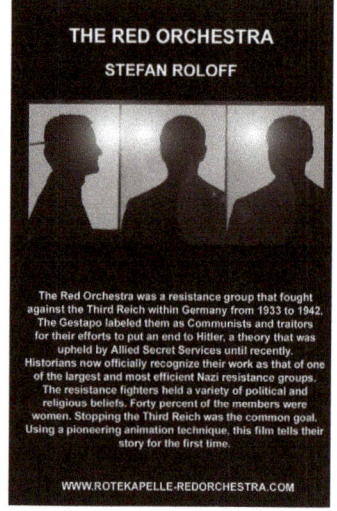

Rosemarie Reed
THE PATH TO NUCLEAR FISSION

*English/German (subtitled)
Run time: 81 minutes; $19.95*

Stefan Roloff
THE RED ORCHESTRA MOVIE DVD

*English/German (subtitled)
Run time: 57 minutes; $24.95*